D1338230

HIDCOTE

The Making of a Garden

HIDCOTE

The Making of a Garden

ETHNE CLARKE

W. W. NORTON & COMPANY

New York • London

For information about permission to reproduce selections from this book, write to
Permissions, W. W. Norton & Company, Inc., 500 Fifth Avenue, New York, NY 10110

For information about special discounts for bulk purchases, please contact W. W. Norton
Special Sales at specialsales@wwnorton.com or 800-233-4830

Manufacturing by Colorprint Offset
Book design by Jonathan D. Lippincott
Production manager: Leeann Graham

Library of Congress Cataloging-in-Publication Data

Clarke, Ethne.
Hidcote : the making of a garden / Ethne Clarke. — 1st American ed.
p. cm.
Original ed. published in 1989.
Includes bibliographical references and index.
ISBN 978-0-393-73267-2 (hardcover)
1. Gardens—England—Gloucestershire. 2. Hidcote Manor Garden
(England) 3. Johnston, Lawrence Waterbury, 1871–1958. I. Title.
II. Title: Making of a garden.
SB466.G8H546 2009
577.5'54094241—dc22
2008053859

ISBN: 978-0-393-73267-2

W. W. Norton & Company, Inc.
500 Fifth Avenue, New York, NY 10110
www.wwnorton.com

W. W. Norton & Company Ltd.
Castle House, 75/76 Wells Street, London W1T 3QT

2 4 6 8 0 9 7 5 3 1

Contents

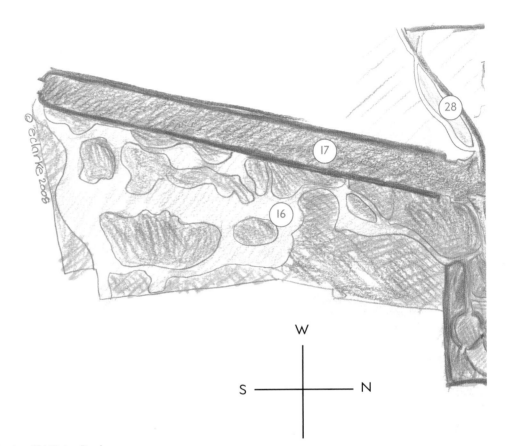

1. Manor House
2. Cedar Lawn
3. Old Garden
4. Circle
5. Red Borders
6. Stilt Garden
7. Maple Garden
8. White Garden
9. Fuchsia Garden
10. Mrs. Winthrop's Garden & Winter Border
11. Alpine Terrace
12. Pillar Garden
13. Rock Bank
14. Stream Garden & Fernery
15. Bathing Pool Garden
16. Wilderness
17. Long Walk
18. Theatre Lawn
19. Beech Avenue
20. Tennis Lawn
21. Rose Walk
22. Summer House (Plant House) & Lily Pool
23. Pine Garden
24. Garden Yard
25. Court Yard
26. Hercules
27. Orchard & Old Kitchen Garden area
28. Lower Stream Garden

W

S —— N

E

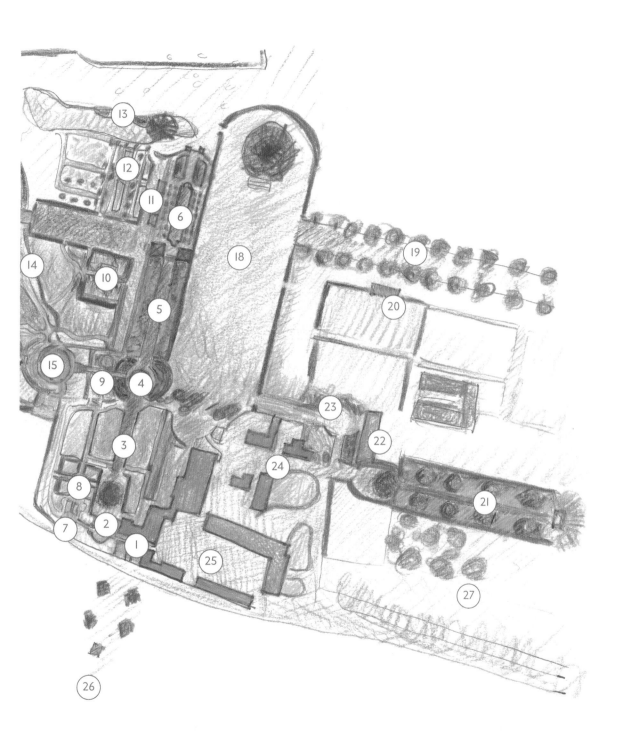

Preface and Acknowledgments

More than twenty years have passed since I researched and wrote the first edition of this book, the first about Major Lawrence Johnston and his garden-making. I was inspired to write it because Johnston was, like me, an American by birth. Yet little mention was made of his American roots—perhaps because Hidcote turned out to be such a seminal garden to English landscape history and his Americanness seemed irrelevant to his creation. And, when I inquired of one of England's leading garden history authorities why there was so little information about him, the answer was "Probably because there is nothing to be known." Looking at the achievement Hidcote represents, his answer was hard to accept; there is always *something* to be learned. And I wanted to know about this mysterious man who made such a bewitching garden.

Hidcote had an enormous impact on me: all those flower-filled garden rooms in which to get lost, to dream about and to be inspired by, which seems to be exactly the impact the place has had on generations of garden-makers and theorists. So the book, like many I have written since, became a dissertation of sorts, the result of my needing to know more about a subject. (A similar drive led me to research the English architect Cecil Pinsent, who made such a lasting impact on the villas and gardens of Tuscany. A contemporary of Johnston, there was little accurately known about him either. Now my research into Pinsent reveals that it's more than likely that the two knew each other.) Research is like a fermenting yeast, expanding the ingredients to make a whole tasty loaf; my research into expatriate gardeners and architects has led me to research better-known expats like Edith Wharton, whose close friendship with Johnston confirmed my assertion that he, like any gardener, did not work in isolation, and that his circle of gardening friends, though small, cast a wide and influential net.

Since I prepared the first edition, the methods of research have changed, and I can now access an incredible amount of information over the Internet that previously I would not have been able to reach without considerable difficulty and expense. Online-research assistance from librarians at Columbia University, New York; The New York Public Library Irma and Paul Milstein Division of United States History, Local History and Genealogy; Royal Botanic Garden, Kew; Department of Plant Science, Oxford University, and from garden experts Jacques Lanteri and Benoit Bourdeau, was helpful beyond measure. Yet I look back wistfully to my earlier round of research, remembering the fine blue onionskin writing paper used by Nancy Lancaster when she wrote to invite me for interviews with her at Haseley Court Coach House, during which she shared her memories of Norah Lindsay and their visits to Hidcote and "Johnnie" (she used lined envelopes and a fountain pen, too). Or recalling my awe-inhibited interview with Graham Stuart Thomas and his candid remarks about his work at the National Trust (when I met him much later at Gravetye Manor, he encouraged me to do another edition; would he have, had he known how I trembled as I rang his doorbell?). I benefited, too, from meeting people who had firsthand knowledge of Johnston, of his mother Gertrude Winthrop, and of members of their family and social set, as well as children of his gardeners and staff. Many are no longer alive, but it was like time travel to listen as they evoked rural life in an England that has all but vanished. Jack Percival, a former gardener at Hidcote, was one of this set. He made contact with me several years after my book was published, and shared with me his experiences and memories of Hidcote and Lawrence Johnston. These memories later guided Glyn Jones in his restoration work, as Jack became a regular visitor and ex-officio garden adviser in the years before his death.

Reviewing their comments now, through the filter of the knowledge and experience I have gained after all the years spent reading and working in the period, has revealed what a novice I was then and how much there was yet to uncover. That is the wonderful thing about research; doors keep opening and new connections are made. Since I wrote the first edition of this book, Johnston's social diaries have been found, and new information has come to light about his genealogy. I am grateful to John Oddy of the Royal Oak Foundation for making available to me several years' worth of genealogical research conducted by William Younger, assisted by Joseph A. Henehan. That was some ten years ago, and Mr. Younger was helping to augment what was known of Johnston since the National Trust was about to launch, at long last, a a systematic conservation program of the garden.

Once again, the staff at Hidcote have been more than helpful, especially the head gardener, Mr. Glyn Jones. The practice of garden renovation has matured, and Mr. Jones has been able, with great sensitivity and thoroughness, to bring the garden back to an appearance its creator might recognize. Serre de la Madone, Johnston's Mediterranean garden in France, has benefited from scholarly work and a rescue program. Once threatened by development, it is now a French national monument, and work there gives us not only hope that the garden will survive, but also an understanding of Johnston's full gardening life, for the two gardens, Hidcote and Serre de la Madone, were two sides of the same coin.

When preparing my first edition, I benefited from the work done by Mr. Seymour Preston and his wife, Mary Alicia, who came again to my assistance through the good offices of their son, Moe Preston, who loaned me his parents' slide collection; some of the images of Hidcote date back to the early 1970s. I'm indebted to the Preston family for the help they have given me with this project and with my first effort. I have benefited from his work and been a little jealous that he had the opportunity to spend such rich times with people who were no longer available to me.

As I write this, the National Trust is celebrating Hidcote Manor Garden's one hundredth anniversary, revealing the garden's facelift. Many of the wrinkles and blemishes I complained about in my first edition have been corrected to the benefit of visitors and the garden's longevity. Funding for this work has been provided in large part by an American with distant ties to Johnston's family. Respecting his desire to remain anonymous, I can say that his gift was prompted by a wish to see Hidcote preserved so that it might continue, as he put it, to inspire and encourage "other people to develop their artistic and practical skills to do more creative and productive tasks in life." It is important to acknowledge the special relationship between our dreams of English gardens and the American "can-do" spirit that so often made them happen, and that this generous gift recognizes the continuing American connections of this most English of English gardens.

Ethne Clarke
Des Moines, Iowa, 2008

Acknowledgment to the First Edition

Lawrence Johnston was not the answer to a garden chronicler's dream: he seems not to have left any diaries, notes, contributions to garden journals, plans, or any of the incunabula associated with the creation of a garden. However, he did leave a collection of memories among the people who knew him directly or indirectly. I am indebted to them for their contributions, so often proffered as being "not very much," but all of which have helped to fill in the picture of the man and his garden:

The Lady Serena James, Sir George Taylor, Sir Anthony Part, Mrs. Nancy Lancaster, Mr. Robin Compton, Mr. James Russell, Mr. Will Ingwersen, Mr. Graham Stuart Thomas, Mr. James Lees-Milne, Mr. John Buxton, Mrs. Primrose Warburg, and Mr. and Mrs. R. Kandiah. Hidcote residents, past and present, were a source of many early memories of Johnston and his garden, and I am deeply grateful for the help I had from Mrs. Margaret Lees (Frank Adams's daughter), Mrs. Bessie Clark ("Pop" Brown's daughter), Misses Ethel, Gladys, and Mary Pearce, and Mrs. M. Gardner (Ted Pearce's nieces and daughter). And thanks to Mr. Ernest Hawkins (Albert Hawkins's brother), Mrs. Madeline Nicholls (Walter Bennett's sister), and Mrs. Brenda Wigram, who brought us all together.

I am extremely grateful to the National Trust for providing me and Andrew Lawson with every facility to visit and photograph in the garden as we desired, and most especially so to Mr. Paul Nicholls, the head gardener, for putting up with my questions and demands for the plant lists, and for sharing my enthusiasm and curiosity about the making of Hidcote. Sir Gawain and Lady Bell deserve my special gratitude for allowing me into their home to gape from the manor windows overlooking the garden. I thank Mr. John Sales for informing me about the Trust's contemporary approach to its stewardship at Hidcote, and Mr. George H. Burrows, former head gardener at Hidcote, for an insight into the Trust's early days with the garden. The efficiency and kindness of the staff of the Registry Office at the National Trust head office made the task of poring over stacks of Hidcote files much easier.

Leads and suggestions provided by Mr. Paul Miles, Mr. William Waterfield, and Mr. Basil Geoffrey-Bolland proved invaluable and opened some interesting avenues of investigation. My thanks are also offered for the help of Mr. R. Thompson of the Regimental Museum, 15/19 King's Royal Hussars, and the librarians and curators of Trinity College Library, the University Botanic Garden, Cambridge, the Royal Botanic Gardens, Edinburgh, the Royal Institute of British Architects, the Landscape Institute, and the London Library.

Details of Johnston's youth were particularly elusive until my cousin-in-law, Diane Schauer, put her genealogical skills to work and scoured the excellent archive facilities available to her through the public records department of the State of Wisconsin Library system, unearthing many pieces of the puzzle. These, combined with the information provided to me by Mr. Seymour Preston, brought the picture into focus, and I owe them both more than I can express. Mr. Preston made available to me the fruits of many years of research into the life of Lawrence Johnston, a pursuit inspired by his and his wife Mary Alicia's love of Hidcote.

This book is for Donald. He said it could be done.

A commemorative fund was established by the friends and customers of Nancy Lindsay to finance the participation of women wishing to accompany plant-hunting expeditions led from Oxford University. The money is held in trust and awarded annually by the Expedition Council through the Oxford Union Exploration Club. Information about the Nancy Lindsay Memorial Fund can be obtained from, and donations sent to: The Office of the Administrator, Department of Plant Sciences, Oxford University, OXON, UK. Quote reference "Source fund B1291."

FOREWORD

Hidcote is still, after half a century, one of the great icons of twentieth-century garden design. Yet its maker, Lawrence Johnston—an expatriate American who became a naturalized Englishman—remains an enigmatic, mysterious figure. The desire to penetrate that presence explains why Ethne Clarke has returned to the subject for a second and much-amplified account of both the garden and its only begetter. Gathered in these pages is as much as we shall ever know about this man who lived to the age of eighty-seven, someone who was born when Queen Victoria still had thirty years before her on the throne and who died when her great-great-granddaughter, Elizabeth II, was in the fifth year of her reign.

Johnston was the obverse of Harold Nicolson—the creator, with his wife, Vita Sackville-West, of Sissinghurst—whose life was one long torrent of the written word. One would think that someone who had lived virtually nine decades would have left more behind him, but no. Like Christopher Lloyd, the plantsman of Great Dixter, Johnston's life was haunted by the spectre of his formidable mother, but in Lloyd's case we have the papers from which to tell the story. We still have practically nothing to round out Johnston's life. Both never formed any partnership, either hetero- or homosexual, although one would guess that both belonged to a generation at a time when any outward leaning in the latter direction would have been suppressed. Both found their salvation in the garden.

Johnston emerges as a stiff, formal, buttoned-up, self-invented, upper-class English country gentleman of his own invention. He longed for a coat of arms which he never got. In the context of his contribution to garden design, the key probably lies in the fact that he read History at Cambridge. That explains the importance of Alicia Amherst's *History of Gardening in England* (1895), which he borrowed several times from the Royal Horticultural Society's Lindley Library. We shall never know if he ever got his own copy, because the National Trust unbelievably sold off his library for £7! What it does establish is that his impulse was to go back, a desire to create in a sense the past and invest himself with the trappings of Merrie England. And the key book there would have been Reginald Blomfield's *The Formal Garden in England* (1892). Hidcote needs to be placed in a line of descent which goes back to the great formal plantings of the Whig aristocracy as recorded in Kip's engravings in *Britannia Illustrata*. Johnston's innovation was to shrink the formula down to a scale affordable to the Edwardian age, just as, later, Rosemary Verey was to shrink it down even further in accordance with the reduced circumstances of late twentieth-century Britain.

I am one of the many who have made the same journey in creating a garden, and my visit to Hidcote was one of the seminal ones. It happened in the winter of 1973–74 on a frosty but sparkling January day when the sky was blue and the light clear on the garden. I have never ceased to be grateful for that visit, for it taught me that if a garden looked amazing in winter it would look good at all the other times of the year. Even more important was learning about a garden's structure and how the architecture—in terms of avenues, vistas, and enclosures of varying sizes and shapes—was crucial to its success. Reading this book I found a strange kinship with Johnston, for he came to gardening at thirty-six and I came to it at thirty-five. Both of us had a strong sense of the past, and the books he read were the ones I too read. Both of us had houses which were architecturally indifferent, but as far as the surrounding domain was concerned the sky was the limit: there was carte blanche. Hidcote is one of the supreme inspirations of what—with flair, imagination, and patience—can be achieved with a bare patch of God's earth.

Roy Strong
The Laskett, Herefordshire, England

Art should be pretty obviously expressed in that part of every garden which is in the immediate vicinity of the House, and may sometimes retain its prominence throughout the whole place.

— Edward Kemp, *How to Lay Out a Garden*, 1850

To an American there is a kind of sanctity even in an English turnip-field, when he thinks how long that small square of ground has been known and recognized as a possession, transmitted from father to son, trodden often by memorable feet, and utterly redeemed from savagery by old acquaintanceship with civilized eyes.

— Nathaniel Hawthorne, *Our Old Home, and English Note-books*, 1891

The garden is a great creation, and should remain an example of what an artist can create with all the plants available to a collector like yourself.

— Lord Aberconway to Lawrence Johnston, November 5, 1948

INTRODUCTION

The English style of garden has long been recognized around the world as the epitome of horticultural good taste. In its various parts or in its entirety, the "English garden" is widely regarded as a model of perfection of the art of gardening.

But what, exactly, is an English garden? At one time, in the late eighteenth and early nineteenth centuries, the English garden meant the studied landscapes of William Kent and Capability Brown. However, though they are still admired and their preservation championed by the horticultural cognoscenti, such gardens no longer move the great gardening public in quite the way that the simple cottage garden does. Sculpted parklands seem today to have less to do with the love of gardening than with some now-obscure literary semaphore, while the cottage garden with its human scale is instantly understood.

Nowadays when garden-lovers turn to their amour, they most frequently embrace gardens made during the first quarter of the twentieth century. These gardens, for all their nostalgic links with the "Golden Afternoon," are created with a veneer of cottage simplicity overlaying the sophistication of layout that was derivative of the Tuscan gardens of Renaissance Italy. The best of these gardens are highly personal creative statements, born of experiment and possessed of great intimacy and sensuality. This is the type of garden that has inspired modern thought, and it was developed from a need to escape the hidebound formulations of what was deemed to be acceptable during the Victorian period—a need that affected most of the arts during that period, from Igor Stravinsky's acknowledged embrace of Renaissance motifs in his early compositions to Ogden Codman and Edith Wharton's *The Decoration of Houses.*

Hidcote is widely acknowledged in gardening circles to be the most influential twentieth-century English garden, in which the disagreements between the "formal" and the "natural" schools of garden design at the turn of the century were resolved, thus setting the course for mainstream garden design and planting for at least the last eighty years. Such is its importance that it was the first garden taken on by the National Trust, in 1948. Today there are more than one hundred gardens under the custodianship of the Trust, whose expertise at preserving the integrity of their properties is a direct result of having to find the ways and means of dealing with a garden that came, unendowed, into its care.

There are other gardens more famous than Hidcote; Sissinghurst is the garden in this category that comes first to most minds. This is hardly surprising, as it has had such a very high profile over the years—there are few people who will not have heard of Vita Sackville-West and Harold Nicolson, the husband-and-wife team who created this garden, beginning in 1938.

But if Hidcote has a low profile, even less is known about Major Lawrence Johnston, the creator of this trendsetting garden. He was an American by birth, part of the "old money" New York society that often, for reasons of economy (and occasionally craving for culture), left the United States to reside in Europe, usually England, France, or Italy. Johnston had some agricultural experience and appears in the 1932 alumni index of Columbia University, New York, as an ungraduated member of the class of 1894, studying "Arch." Presumably architecture, not archeology. But it's doubtful this amounted to a full course of study, and he evidently did not have any formal horticultural training.

Major Johnston did have a painter's eye, however, and was in many respects a talented artist. He also was used to having, and expected to have, the best of everything. So he was able to utilize his own and other people's abilities to his advantage. He was unhindered by preconceived notions of garden design and by what was perceived as acceptable horticultural practice. He was an American in love with his English heritage, and these qualities, combined with his discerning taste, no doubt enabled him to distill the essence of English style and create a garden *sans surpasse*.

This book also examines the influences at play in the world of garden design at the end of the nineteenth and beginning of the twentieth centuries. This includes the work of formalists in landscape and architecture, which gave rise to an argument—the so-called "Battle of the Styles"—between the most vociferous exponents of that practice, the architects Reginald Blomfield and J. D. Sedding, and the self-anointed arbiter of English gardening, William Robinson. Within that historical framework can be traced the development and later influences of Hidcote Manor, and the motivations and history of its creator.

Major Lawrence Johnston, detail of photograph. See page 31.

One

THE EARLY YEARS

In July 1907, the wealthy American widow Gertrude Winthrop purchased the farm of Hidcote Bartrim at an auction sale conducted at the Noel Arms Hotel in Chipping Campden. After years of country-hopping between the United States, France, and England, she settled on a property that would provide not only a peaceful haven for her closing years, but an estate and enterprise for her cherished son, Lawrence. The farm had nearly three hundred acres and a village of seven cottages, a blacksmith, and a small population to provide estate workers.

Lawrence's parents were independently wealthy American expatriates. His father, Elliott Johnston, was born in Baltimore, Maryland, on May 1, 1826. The Johnstons were a prominent banking family trading after the Civil War as Johnston Brothers & Co. at 198 Baltimore Street in that city; a circular advertised their services as including being able to "draw sterling exchange and francs, in sums to suit."

From 1861 to 1865, the United States was torn apart by the Civil War, and while the State of Maryland was nominally pro-Union, the genuine sympathies of many of the state's citizens lay with the Confederacy. This possibly explains why Elliott, who had been a midshipman and first lieutenant at the Naval Academy in Annapolis, Maryland, served in the Confederate forces on the staff of General Richard Stoddard Ewell. But apart from possible family allegiances to the South, Elliott might also have been influenced by the twelve years he spent sometime before the outbreak of war as a planter on the Eastern Shore of Virginia.

That the Johnston family enjoyed a considerable degree of social standing in the pre–Civil War years is illustrated by the fact that Elliott's sister-in-law, his brother Henry's wife, was Harriet Lane, whose uncle, James Buchanan, was the fifteenth president of the United States, immediately preceding Abraham Lincoln. Since Buchanan was unmarried, Harriet served as the First Lady in his White House and, before his election, had acted as his official hostess when he was the United States ambassador to the Court of St. James's. While in London, Harriet established herself prominently in the social scene as she was especially favored by Queen Victoria—a rare honor.

The Civil War, however, does not seem to have damaged the Johnstons' social credibility or to have caused the family too much long-standing resentment toward the Union, because five years after the end of the war, Elliott married Gertrude Cleveland Waterbury, the daughter of a wealthy northern family whose roots ran deep into American history. Gertrude was descended on her father's side from John Waterbury, a founder of Connecticut. Born in England in 1615, by 1646, Waterbury had emigrated to the American colonies, where he settled at Stamford, Connecticut. A later ancestor, General David Waterbury, was on George Washington's staff during the Revolutionary War. Gertrude's grandfather was a founder of the First National Bank of Brooklyn. On her mother's side, Gertrude claimed descent from Moses Cleveland, who migrated from Ipswich, Suffolk, England, about 1635, to Woburn, Massachusetts. This ancestry gave the family irreproachable social standing, and her family's success in business made Gertrude heiress to a not-insignificant fortune.

Gertrude was born on December 21, 1845, the second daughter of Lawrence Waterbury and Caroline Cleveland. She had two sisters: Julia (two years older) and Catherine (three years younger, who later became the wife of J. Pierpont Edwards, the British consul to New York City from 1861 to 1882). The youngest member of the family was James Montaudevert, born when Gertrude was six years old (and whose later flamboyance as a "club man"—there was hardly a New York club to which he did not belong—was matched only by his profligate ways with the Waterbury inheritance). Their father was founder (in 1845) and proprietor of T. Waterbury & Co., manufacturers of cordage of all kinds—binder twine, jute rope, and wool twine, manila paper, and bagging for baling cotton—a prosaic enough enterprise, and one that would have been able to turn a profit even during the Civil War, with certain of their products much in demand. He later established two profitable ferry companies, and in time became the director of the First National Bank of Brooklyn, founded by his father. At his death, he left an estate of more than $2 million and, as a friend said, "not an enemy in the world."

On Thursday, October 20, 1870, when she was twenty-five and he was forty-four years old, Gertrude married Elliott at St. Peter's Church, Westchester, New York, from her father's residence, Pleasance, also in Westchester. The name of the house, a medieval term for "garden," causes one to wonder if the main focus of the property was indeed its garden. In later years, Gertrude was known for her love of plants and her skill as a gardener.

On November 21, 1870, Elliott Johnston received the passport he had applied for three days earlier; it included his wife Gertrude, and with that the Johnstons moved to France. Elliott may have been looking after the family's foreign exchange interests, or it may be that, like many other Americans whose wealth had been depleted by the post–Civil War depreciation of the national currency, they found it cheaper to live in Europe, where, as Edith Wharton once remarked, many went to economize. Although Gertrude was an heiress, her husband's fortune had yet to be made. He came from a good family and was a disabled war veteran; in 1865, Elliott Johnston is recorded, in a history of Confederate staff officers, to have traveled to Europe. It is said that he went in search of a better-quality prosthesis, having lost his left leg in 1862 at Sharpsburg (aka the Battle of Antietam), where he was taken prisoner by Union forces. In November 1863, he declared himself unfit for duty and retired to the Invalid Corps in December 1864.

Whatever their reasons for moving, the couple soon began their own family. They were in Paris for the birth of their first child, Lawrence Waterbury, who arrived on October 12, 1871, just eight days before his parents' first wedding anniversary. Nine months later, on July 15, 1872, at Montier, Switzerland, their second son, Elliott, Jr., was born. The following year, on January 22, Gertrude sailed from Liverpool, England, to New York; Elliott followed in September. Neither roster lists the children, which is unusual since dependents' names are routinely recorded after the main traveler's name. At some point, the family returned to Europe, to Nice in the south of France, possibly to provide a kinder climate for the confinement of an exhausted Gertrude and the birth of their third child. Named after her paternal grandmother, Elizabeth, she arrived just in time for Christmas, on December 22, 1873, but lived for only seven months, dying at Ferney (on the French–Swiss border) in July 1874. On July 6 that year, Elliott traveled alone to the United States. One year later, in September, he made the same journey. The Johnstons were not, on the evidence, a settled family, and their constant peregrinations across Europe and the Atlantic must have been wearing, not to mention expensive.

How long after this first personal tragedy the Johnstons remained in France is uncertain, but in 1880 the Federal Census for New York records Elliott, Gertrude, and their two sons in residence at 66 East 35th Street, along with a twenty-five-year-old black servant, James Hoffman, and twenty-two-year-old Marie Franz, listed as a boarder, but since she was French, Marie was probably there as a governess or French tutor for the boys.

By then, Lawrence was nine years old, his brother Elliott eight. In New York, they were surrounded by numerous Waterbury cousins; his uncle James had eight children, two of whom, James Montgomery ("Monte") and Lawrence ("Larry"), became international polo stars and often played in England during the early 1900s, while their cousin was busy at Hidcote.

Wealthy American families of this period were exceptionally close and moved within a tight social bracket. There can be little doubt that Lawrence and his brother were soon firmly established in the extensive Waterbury clan. Lawrence's life thus far had been unsettled, shuttling to and fro between the United States and Europe, and living at a different address each time the family returned to New York. What could have been more pleasurable when arriving as a virtual immigrant in your own country than to be accepted into a gaggle of younger cousins and caring aunts and uncles?

Presumably, the extended family offered the Elliott Johnstons some support. It might also have gone some way toward easing Lawrence's pain from losing his father, sometime in the mid-1880s, for it appears from census records that Gertrude and Elliott were no longer living together. She is listed alone as Mrs. Elliott Johnston in the Trow Directory, and the Social Registers show her living with her sons. Elliott seems to disappear completely from the scene until he reappears in a 1900 Federal Census record as the head of a household in Pungoteague, Accomack County, Virginia. His age is recorded as seventy-four, married for thirteen years to a woman whose name was given as Alice M., aged thirty-three. That would have them marrying about 1887, when she was twenty and he was sixty-three.

Historically, the New York legislature authorized divorce, but only for adultery, and that did not change until 1966. Divorce was shamefully unacceptable for someone of Gertrude's caste (it took Edith Wharton nearly a decade to begin divorce proceedings against her husband, Teddy, who made "arrangements" to be caught in a compromising situation with a woman who was not his wife, after which Edith lived exclusively abroad). But until a record of the dissolution of the Johnston's marriage is found, the cause can only be guessed. Curiously, on September 8, 1875, Elliott and the boys traveled on the *Bothnia* from New York to Liverpool with a woman named Jane, who the ship's purser identified as Elliott's wife.

Gertrude's response to the change in her status is unknown (subsequent news clippings in which she is mentioned refer to her as a widow of Elliott Johnston, but her sister Julia's will refers to her as "formerly" married to Elliott Johnston). What is certain is that, throughout her life, Gertrude kept Lawrence on a short rein.

One can only imagine the effect this must have had on Lawrence at that impressionable age; losing his father under what most certainly were strained circumstances must have left the boy feeling orphaned emotionally. It has been said that children who regard themselves as orphans feel like ugly ducklings, uncomfortable with people who have had a stable upbringing in a complete family, and, most significantly, alone in the world. Some people never shake off the burden of their grief, with the result that their adult development is crippled by the fear of repeated loss; others use it as a source of enormous creative energy, fashioning their own security. Both these aspects can be seen in Johnston's later life. The gardens he created are his only testimony, and the people who knew him claim they never really knew him at all, that he was diffident, eschewed celebrity, and always maintained a distance between himself and those who came within his orbit.

Johnston wrote in a letter that he had been raised largely in France, but that is not to say that his Continental upbringing was continuous. The New York City Trow Directory for 1882–83 lists the Johnstons as resident in New York. In 1887, only Gertrude is listed in the Directory and in the Social Register, but without an address, which may indicate that she and her sons were not living in New York. They may have been in Paris, since Gertrude's sister and brother-in-law were in that city early in 1887, and returned to New York on February 19. Lawrence, Elliott, Jr., and Gertrude would certainly have been in London on November 5, 1887, the day Gertrude remarried. Her second husband was Charles Francis Winthrop, eighteen years her senior and a prominent barrister from New York City.

Winthrop's family was as well placed as his new wife's, and in fact there is every chance that they knew each other while she was still married to Elliott Johnston, since they belonged to the same New York clubs as Gertrude's father, uncle, and brother. Later in his life, Lawrence was a frequent visitor to Edith Wharton's home, Château Sainte-Claire, in the hills above Hyères in the south of France, but their friendship may well have originated in his youth. Edith's great friend was Egerton Leigh Winthrop, Lawrence's stepfather's second cousin. Egerton also belonged to many of the same clubs as Lawrence's grandfather and uncles and lived on East 31st Street, just a few blocks from where the Johnstons were living in 1880. With her marriage to Winthrop, Gertrude maintained her social position and enhanced financial security for herself and Lawrence.

In England, 1890, Lawrence began preparation for university entrance and became a student at a "crammer," where the possibly sketchy early education of privately tutored young people was brought to a finer pitch. In Lawrence's case, this was achieved by John Dunn, a former scholar and M.A. of St. John's College, Cambridge, who took resident pupils at his home in the village of Little Shelford, south of Cambridge.

Lawrence was under his tuition for four years, and on October 22, 1894, he enrolled as a pensioner at Trinity College, Cambridge, pensioner being the middle of the three social groups in which undergraduates were classified at matriculation to the university. The college has no record of his subsequent scholastic career other than that in 1897 he was awarded a B.A. with a second-class degree in history; his exams included English Constitutional History and the History of the Papacy.

At the same time that Lawrence appears in the student roles at Cambridge, there is an indication, from the alumni lists of Columbia College (published in 1932) that he and his brother Elliott were enrolled, respectively, in the architecture department and the engineering department. Columbia's architecture program was only newly launched in 1894, the year the record shows that Johnston should have graduated, with Elliott graduating the following year. Neither of them actually did. It may be that they were enrolled simply to follow family tradition, as most Waterbury men were Columbia men, or they may have been keeping a foothold in their paternal country. However, Lawrence listed his profession as engineer when traveling from England to America in June 1895 aboard the steamer *Furst Bismarck*. He may have benefited from exposure to formal architectural training as Columbia's program was designed to groom young men to study at the École des Beaux-Arts in Paris, while at Cambridge University, Lawrence's history studies would certainly have brought him into contact with the artistic traditions of Renaissance Italy and England, which were later to inspire the architecture and garden design at a time when these concerns were Johnston's primary interest. Although Johnston's architectural studies were putative rather than substantiated, there is no doubt that he possessed an innate sense of good taste and an unerring eye for quality and ability in both the people who became his friends and the plants he was to nurture. Lawrence was a talented amateur artist, but that was a side of his nature that developed only after he came to Hidcote.

Lawrence's student years at Cambridge must have been a relatively quiet, settled time in contrast to his usual peripatetic existence, shuffling between his mother's home in New York, various French cities, and presumably London. Then, on January 25, 1900, at Cornhill-on-Tweed, Northumberland, Lawrence took steps to tie himself even more closely to the country where he seems to have at last felt a sense of belonging, by becoming a naturalized British citizen. He promptly enlisted in the British army to fight in the Boer War in South Africa. On February 2, 1900, 3296 Private Johnston, Lawrence, 15th (Northumberland and Durham) Company of the 5th Battalion Imperial Yeomanry sailed for

South Africa aboard the SS *Monteagle*; he was embarking on a military career that was to span the next twenty years. Joining the armed forces of his adopted country effectively ended his citizenship in the United States. He may well have had an ulterior motive in enlisting, as army service would be bound to take him away from his mother's smothering devotion, which no doubt increased when her second husband died in 1898. Escaping to battle may seem a fairly drastic step to take, but he was nearing thirty and may have felt it was time to strike out for independence, to establish himself on his own terms.

Lawrence served in South Africa for one year. According to a report in the *Illustrated Chronicle*, October 27, 1914, he "took part in the operations of Cape Colony, North of the Orange River, including the action at Ruidam, and also in the fighting in Orange River colony and the Transvaal. He received the Queen's South Africa Medal with three clasps and the King's South African Medal with two clasps."

It was during this year that Lawrence met George Savile Clayton, who became an influential friend. Savile Clayton was a lieutenant in the 14th (Northumberland and Durham) Company of Johnston's battalion; his family had been officers in the Northumberland Hussars from 1886. A photograph taken in South Africa in 1900 shows Savile Clayton: dark-haired and strong-featured, with a luxuriant mustache, his shirt-sleeves rolled up and completely at ease. He gives the impression of being the exact physical opposite of young Lawrence, who was short, had thinning fair hair above a high forehead, mild blue eyes, and a small speech impediment that made him pronounce all his *r*'s as *v*'s. He also suffered from "weak lungs" (a nonspecific affliction that drew many young men to Africa; one yeomanry private was a doctor who joined when he discovered a suspected TB patch on his lungs).

Perhaps Savile Clayton was everything that young Lawrence aspired to be: an English military gentleman with a family history of service to a single regiment. For in the years following his service in the Boer War, Lawrence rose steadily through the ranks, his postings and promotions announced in the *London Gazette* and his photo appearing in the *Daily Graphic* under the headline "*The Nation's Roll of Honour*" when he was wounded during the First World War.

Although Johnston may have been acquiring the trappings of an English gentleman, he was still on the move, his army career taking him

Major Lawrence Johnston, the American
Hidcote Manor Gardens in 1907

The obscure and little-known American, Lawrence Johnston, who created Hidcote
Manor Gardens, peers out from behind a corner of the hedge framing the Theatre Lawn,
c. 1948. He never liked being photographed.

from Aldershot for the first six months of 1903 to Hythe for a brief
period in 1905 as he pursued the courses that meant promotion. He also
made two trips back to the United States, in January and December
1905. Each time, he traveled with a valet (or they may have been his bat-
men—enlisted servants): two brothers, twenty-seven-year-old Ernest
Carham, and his older brother, twenty-nine-year-old Edward.

Throughout his life, Lawrence took pains to travel in style and comfort and to embrace the lifestyle of a landed English country gentleman.
The two things he lacked to complete his transformation were land and
a family pedigree. The first was to prove easier to acquire than the latter.

Lawrence engaged a London solicitor, A. M. Burke, to trace his
Johnston ancestry, and in July 1906, Burke wrote to Lawrence at Little

The manor house at Hidcote in 1907 before Johnston moved the main entrance to the side of the house and blocked access from the lane running through the village.

This view from the gazebo platform looks along the double perennial borders toward the cedar of Lebanon and the manor house. Note the predominant use of grasses in the border.

Shelford (Gertrude may have stayed on living there while Lawrence pursued his army career) with the results of his searches.

Americans have always been preoccupied by their origins, but this was more than curiosity. Lawrence was trying to construct a heritage that would set his foot firmly on the rungs of the English social ladder. He was, after all, nothing more than the son of rich Americans—even the adoption of British nationality and valiant service in the armed forces would not give the kind of social credibility he wished for. But the Johnston family had Irish antecedents, as attested by a letter written by Lawrence's great-great-grandfather stating that in 1753 he and his wife had emigrated from Dublin to Philadelphia. The Irish connection certainly compounded the difficulty of tracing Johnston's pedigree. Even more disappointing for Lawrence was the news that came to him in Little Shelford from Mr. Burke in a letter dated June 11, 1906: "Throughout the enquiry I have given particular attention to the question of armorial bearings but unfortunately none of the documents, wills, etc., relating to the family throw any light on this point." Eventually, Burke determined that John Johnston (nicknamed Old Lurg) was an ancestor and supplied a drawing of arms. It is curious that Lawrence didn't try to give equal emphasis to his English, Waterbury ancestors, who were notably more prestigious than his father's Irish family. Why Lawrence didn't pursue his mother's pedigree is not known: would he have had to change his last name to adopt any armorial bearings that turned up, or was it just part of his oedipal complexities that made him turn away from her line? In any case, he most likely would have stood a better chance of coming up with something impressive by researching the Waterburys rather than the Johnstons. And the coat of arms seen above the entrance to the manor today was apparently already in place when Gertrude purchased the manor.

Just after 1900, when he wasn't on military duty, Lawrence lodged with a Northumberland landowner named George Bay and began to study farming at Humshaugh, near Hexham, the village near which the Savile Claytons lived. In July 1907, Gertrude purchased the estate of Hidcote Bartrim at auction. The new insurance for Hidcote was effected through the Newcastle branch of Lawrence's Hexham insurance company.

The property included nearly three hundred acres, a village of seven cottages, a blacksmith, and a farmhouse that had been severely damaged by fire and rebuilt in the early 1800s. There was no garden as such, just a collection of rose beds and cabbages and an enormous cedar of Lebanon.

In the beginning, Gertrude was the keen gardener and Lawrence, when home, took an interest in managing the farm. This soon altered, for it became apparent that Lawrence's talents lay elsewhere. He was not a dedicated farmer, and the garden may have attracted him because it offered more of an outlet for his artistic skills. The farm was handed over to a manager and the garden became Lawrence's domain.

Today, if one stops on the road below Hidcote and considers its position in relation to the village of Mickleton below, it brings to mind the siting of a Tuscan villa set on the highest level with the *podere*, or home farm, coming right up to the boundary walls that enclose the villa garden. Perhaps Lawrence saw this potential and considered that he could build his own private estate, with the people of the hamlet to provide the services required by the manor house; staff were drawn from the families living in the cottages that lined the narrow grass-edged track that led through the hilltop village, and also from the villagers living at Mickleton at the foot of the hill.

One of the earliest employees at Hidcote was Edward (Ted) Pearce. He was out of work in the autumn of 1907 when Johnston moved into the manor. They met by chance, and Lawrence asked Pearce if he would help him with clearing the garden—just for a few weeks. Fifty-three years later, Pearce was still there. This is typical of the kind of loyalty Lawrence and Gertrude inspired in the people who worked for them; a loyalty that lived on in the children and surviving relatives of their staff, who all remembered the generosity and solicitude shown by the Major and most especially by "Madame Winthrop," as she was known to those who worked for her.

Gertrude was a petite woman with a stern manner and piercing blue eyes that could silence an unruly child at ninety paces, particularly when sighted through her lorgnette. She was deeply involved with the welfare of the Hidcote staff and especially concerned with the health and spiritual well-being of the children of the estate. Madame Winthrop organized Salvation Army meetings in one of the outbuildings at the manor and each Sunday would march down the lane gathering the children to ensure their attendance. She was a committed Christian, raised as an

Episcopalian, and even in her old age would walk across the fields to Mickleton for services in the village church.

Christmas parties organized by Gertrude and given in the hall of the manor provided the children of Hidcote and Mickleton with an extravagant treat. There were cakes, sausages, sweets, jellies, Christmas crackers, a huge Christmas tree, and entertainers; on one occasion she arranged for a stilt-walker from a traveling fun fair to put in an appearance. This apparition so terrified Bessie Brown, the daughter of Johnston's batman, "Pop" Brown, who also served as Madame Winthrop's butler, that she started crying. "Come over here, you silly little girl, and sit by me," was the command, which only compounded the child's unhappiness since Bessie was thoroughly frightened by Madame Winthrop's stern countenance.

Gertrude Johnston Winthrop, née Waterbury, Lawrence Johnston's mother in her dotage. She was from an old New York family and independently wealthy; she purchased Hidcote Manor c. 1925.

Bessie recalled that as a child she had suffered poor health and so was a focus of Gertrude's attentions, and had always to sit by her at church services so that Madame could keep a better eye on her.

Mary Pearce and her sisters Gladys and Ethel were also raised at Hidcote. Their father was a shepherd on the farm and Johnston's head gardener, Ted Pearce, was their uncle. When Mary was christened, the choice of name upset Madame Winthrop, who felt she should have been named Gertrude. So the next child was named Gladys Gertrude, but the family joke was that this upset Madame even more, but not enough to dull her fondness of the little girl. Gladys recalls how, having being told off by her granny, Madame found her in tears and took her off in the chauffeur-driven car to play with the children of a neighboring county family while Madame conducted her visit. In 1910, Gertrude traveled to Italy. She managed to keep in touch with events at Hidcote, though, and sent a postcard from Rome to the girls' mother congratulating her on the birth of another child.

No doubt Gertrude's concern for the village children was rooted in the death so long ago of her daughter Elizabeth. Her middle child, Elliott, Jr., was living independently and her treasured oldest child was growing away from her. The more she tried to protect and bind him to her, the further he withdrew, not just from her, but from staff and others who were close to him. As he grew older, Lawrence Johnston became ever more diffident, shying away from any kind of attention; in the few photographs of him that survive, he averts his eyes or turns his back to the camera. The only memory common to all the grown-up children of Hidcote was that he was rarely there and that when he was, he was rarely seen, which they attributed to the growing friction between Lawrence and his mother.

Throughout the years in which Hidcote was being developed, Lawrence continued his army service. In 1909, he was promoted to captain and in 1913 was given a leave of absence, from February 5 to April 5, with permission to travel abroad, specifically to "Egypt and the Courts of Italy." The Waterburys were a large family, and one of Lawrence's cousins, Reginald K. Waterbury, traveled to Italy at the end of December 1914, visiting "relatives" in England en route to Milan, where he planned to study music. He joined the expatriate members of his family and, after serving in the Red Cross during the First World War, became the secretary of the American Chamber of Commerce in Milan and then worked for Texas-based cotton importers at their Milan office. He returned to live in the United States in the 1930s, perhaps to avoid involvement in the approaching war. (He died in 1972 at his residence on Staten Island.) Given the closeness of the Waterbury clan, there can be little doubt that Lawrence and Reginald were close and visited each other during their expatriate years.

In May 1913, Lawrence was attached to the 12th Lancers, and one year later the first mention of him with the rank of major appears on regimental orders dated May 22, 1914. The First World War started one month later, and in August he was Officer Commanding "A" Squadron at Gosforth Park; in September he was the officer in charge of transport when the Northumberland Hussars moved from Gosforth to Lyndhurst, Hampshire; and on October 23, in the area of Hooge Château, Johnston was wounded.

There is no record in the military history of the Northumberland Hussars of the severity of Johnston's injury, although the appendix states that he was wounded twice. It is reputed that on one of these occasions he was taken for dead and laid out for burial, but an acquaintance attached to the burial detail was doubly astonished to recognize the corpse of someone he knew and then to see the supposed corpse twitch. Johnston recovered from his wounds and was back in service as second-in-command of the regiment in June 1916, and then served as temporary commanding officer of the Hussars for most of February 1917.

After the war, in 1920, the Northumberland Hussars were one of the ten Yeomanry Regiments retained from the original fifty-six. Major Lawrence Johnston rejoined as second-in-command on May 21, 1920. After that date, there is no further mention of him taking an active role in the service of his regiment, so it must be assumed that he retired to the reserves having acquitted himself honorably in the service of his adopted country. Setting Johnston's military career against his later life suggests that exposure to battle considerably shaped his personality. The Boer War was marked by atrocities on both sides, and without delving into the history of that conflict, it is sufficient to acknowledge that Lawrence experienced the suffering, either firsthand or from a distance. Similarly, the First World War was, even at the time, recognized for its brutality and its decimation of an entire generation—the brightest and best—and Lawrence himself twice came near to being one of the lost. While he fought and served loyally, he also had a sensitive nature, and Hidcote may well have represented a refuge from the mayhem he had witnessed.

Johnston's military career had eclipsed the development of the gardens at Hidcote, and in fact, during the four years of his active service, much that he had achieved in the seven years from 1907 had fallen into disarray, so that work had virtually to begin again. But now he was free to concentrate on the garden that was to become his life's obsession. As one area of the garden was completed, a new idea took hold, requiring more land and more money, causing his farm manager to despair over the loss of profitable farmland and his mother to lament the demands of her extravagant son.

Lawrence's younger brother, Elliott, was 40 years old when he died on March 16, 1912 in Fullerton, California. He was buried twelve days later in his mother's plot in Woodlawn Cemetery, New York, which she had purchased in 1904. He is the sole occupant of the grave; the name Winthrop is cut into its base and it is marked with a Celtic cross. Researcher William Younger, who uncovered this and a considerable amount of other family information, described Elliott's resting place "all rather forlorn and melancholy."

At the time of writing, I was unable to recover Elliott, Jr.'s death certificate, but an item in the *New York Times*, October 20, 1914, shows that Elliott Johnston & Co., Inc. Guaranteed Waterproofing and Construction Co. was named as a debtor to the East River National Bank for $2,576.00 in a judgment filed in New York County Court. Was this Lawrence's brother? The profession fits; had he gone west to remake his life in California as so many did at that time? With just one child left to worry about, the widow Winthrop turned her full attention on him. Her main concern about "Lawrie" was, in her terms, his complete lack of financial sensibility, which was to become a source of endless irritation between them. He resented having to rely on her for money, and she kept a tight hold on the purse strings. However, Lawrie usually got his way, and the garden flourished.

Johnston's success as a garden designer preceded by some years his acumen as a plantsman. He had no formal horticultural schooling, and likewise no practical training in architecture. Like his neighbor Mr. Flowers, who was creating a beautiful house and garden at Ilmington Manor, on the other side of the hill from Hidcote, he was an informed amateur with an artistic ability and the determination to utilize it. Such people are willing to seek expert advice, hiring architects, landscape designers, and so on, but remain convinced of their own talents, using the professional only as a sounding board or whipping boy.

Lawrence was an amateur painter. At Hidcote, there is a painting by him of a floral bouquet composed of blossoms gathered from the garden; this painting was a gift for his friends the Muirs who lived and gardened at neighboring Kiftsgate Court. Mrs. Nancy Lancaster, who was a guest at Hidcote on several occasions, recalls that the room she stayed in was hung with huge canvases, painted by Johnston like "tapestry maquettes," on which were depicted views of the garden, "rather like the map of the garden at Port Lympne," painted by Rex Whistler for its owner, Sir Philip Sassoon, one of Johnston's numerous society friends. In his own room, situated over what is now the tea room, on the wall immediately to the right of the large bay window that looks out over the Old Garden, Johnston is said to have painted exactly the view he could see, rather like René Magritte's painting *La Condition Humaine,* of the artist's easel in front of a window (renovation work has not revealed any trace of this). He may have got his fondness for murals from his close friend, the erstwhile garden designer and artist Aubrey Waterfield, who also painted murals, contributing one to Kiftsgate. (With his wife Lina, Waterfield lived in the ruined fortress of Aulla in Italy. Lina's aunt, Janet Ross, was the owner of Poggio Gherardo in Settignano, near Florence, and mentor to the expat community in Tuscany.)

Johnston's artistic leanings also extended to interior décor. He collected antiques, particularly seventeenth-century English furniture, Delft tiles and Chinese porcelain, and gardening paraphernalia. Among his treasures were two eighteenth-century watering cans that had been used at Versailles and a copper watering can that was thought to be seventeenth-century Italian. In all, Lawrence worked to make Hidcote's amenities as modern and comfortable as he could beneath a veneer of dignified age and the appearance of inherited estate. For example, Lawrence once purchased a new carpet for his rooms, but decided that the blue was too strident and so had the carpet vigorously washed and put out of doors to weather and fade before he would admit it to the décor. To his staff, this behavior seemed eccentric, but it is indicative of an artistic temperament and shows that Johnston had the patience and determination to get precisely the effect he was after—traits common to many accomplished designers.

He could play the piano well and was a keen and accomplished tennis player. The tennis court at Hidcote had been reinstated, and his house parties were often organized around tennis, when he would employ a professional coach for the benefit of his guests. There were also separate courts for badminton and squash, created within the outbuildings surrounding the courtyard. The National Trust intends to hold tennis parties once again at Hidcote; as Graham Stuart Thomas once remarked, few sounds are more redolent of English country gardens than the "thwack" of a tennis racquet hitting a ball across a grass court.

Johnston has been described by those who knew him and worked with him as a "stiff little man," "formal," "proper," and as a demanding employer who, although prepared to listen to the opinions of others, would always expect things to be done the way he wanted them done and would readily show his displeasure if they were not. Curiously, he was, at the same time, cordial with the men in his employ and would involve them in his decision-making processes rather than just hand out the orders. Ted Pearce recalled to his niece, "He was a decent sort of man, and if you satisfied him, he would pat you on the shoulder and say it was good, or if he saw anything special in the garden . . . which he thought was a lovely piece of work, he would come and fetch you to look at it." Though he enjoyed the trappings of one, he never, however, played the "lord of the manor" to the people on whom he relied.

Friends of Johnston's have said that he worked alongside his gardeners; however, those who worked for him said he never actually dirtied his hands, and that he was content to direct his staff and oversee the jobs at hand, ensuring that they were properly done. But as the garden grew in size and stature, Johnston became aware that he needed a second-in-command, so in 1922 he hired his first professionally trained gardener, Frank Adams.

It was Johnston's talent always to select the best, and in appointing a head gardener he no doubt realized that he required a man with a wide range of practical horticultural skills that would perfectly com-

Lawrence Johnston and head gardener Frank Adams, who was with him the longest and was instrumental in the shaping of Hidcote's planting. Johnston is petting Timmy; Ricky waits his turn; Johnston always kept dogs. c. 1927.

plement his own considerable abilities as the garden designer and connoisseur of fine plants he had become, a man on whom he could rely to do what was necessary without having to be told. Adams had been a gardener for King George V, in charge of the flower decoration at Windsor Castle, just the sort of credentials Lawrence would have been looking for—in every respect.

Two

HIDCOTE BARTRIM MANOR

When Lawrence Johnston began the gardens at Hidcote, he was working with a clean slate. The only features of any interest were the stately cedar of Lebanon directly behind the house and a stand of beech trees to the west. The terrain sloped roughly from north to south, with the property sited on a ridge and buffeted by the winds from all sides. The soil was mediocre, tending to be heavy and alkaline.

It is not possible to say definitely what attracted Gertrude and Lawrence to the Cotswolds. It probably had more to do with logistics than anything else, since she and Lawrence and his brother Elliott, who was also listed as being resident at Hidcote, were shuttling back and forth from England to America, and their most frequently used ports were Liverpool and Southampton, both easier to reach from the West Country than from remote East Anglia. The sampling of agriculture may already have given him a taste for gardening, and had he wished to pursue the farming life, he would presumably have been better off in the expanses of northern England or Cambridgeshire and East Anglia, which have long been recognized as the most productive agricultural areas in England. But neither the rugged north of England nor the characterless fenlands around Cambridgeshire spring to mind if one is considering garden-making. Perhaps he and Gertrude just grew tired of the cold and found the comparative warmth and gentler climate of Gloucestershire and the west of England more alluring. When they

Lawrence Johnston, c. 1935; one of the few full-face portraits of this enigmatic man.

arrived in the Vale of Evesham to take up residence at Hidcote, Gertrude was sixty-two years old and Lawrence thirty-six.

Or, the reason for their choice might have been that, by the early 1900s, the Cotswolds had become a fashionable place to live, particularly among the artistic community, who were drawn to the mellow stone manors and cottages in the villages Chipping Campden and Broadway. It was a cosmopolitan society composed of sophisticated, well-educated, and often well-heeled people who were seeking similar company. Nearby was Stanway House, with its picturesque water garden designed by Charles Bridgeman. From 1883, Stanway had been the home of Lord and Lady Elcho. The latter, née Mary Wyndham, was an energetic hostess who made Stanway the spiritual home of the Souls, a social group drawn from the ranks of the English aristocracy and united in their pursuit of the aesthetic life. They were the beautiful people of the turn of the century—young, talented, and wealthy. Patrons of the Arts and Crafts designers, they were themselves amateur painters, poets, and sculptors.

"Broadway is a place of complete freedom. It has no sharp conventional corners. Mental staylacing is unknown, and everyone is as free and easy as in bedroom slippers," wrote Mary Anderson de Navarro, one of the greatest actresses of the Victorian era and an American expatriate whose circle of friends included Henry James (who, along with Edith Wharton, was an "honorary Soul"), Surrey-based artist and sculptor G. F. Watts and his wife Mary, Sir Lawrence Alma-Tadema, and eventually Lawrence Johnston. Anderson's talents were widely admired, and the actress was as well known for the perfection of her garden as for her stage performances.

Lawrence and Gertrude were moderately artistic but widely traveled, and the breadth of their experience was evident in their appreciation of fine things. The intellectual atmosphere and the presence of the Arts and Crafts patrons and practitioners may well have offered them more attractive social opportunities than were available in the remoter reaches of England, where more prosaic rural pursuits such as fox hunts and pheasant shoots were the norm. It was, by comparison, a setting more conducive to creative expression. The architect Charles E. Ashbee (Lawrence's contemporary at Cambridge) relocated his Guild of Handicraft in 1902 to Chipping Campden in the Cotswolds; at Broad Campden, Ashbee adapted the historic Norman Chapel for the art historian Ananda Coomaraswamy, a friend of William Morris. At the start of his career, Morris was strongly allied with the Pre-Raphaelite Brotherhood, and their leaning toward Gothicism had led him, in the 1860s, to try to recreate a medieval garden at his home, Red House, near Bexleyheath in Surrey, using wattle fencing to create small "rooms" furnished with lilies, old roses, topiary, and dovecotes. But, so attractive were the Cotswolds that Morris, the leading light of the Arts and Crafts Movement, had in the later years of his life lived in Broadway Tower.

Morris had established a furnishing company that relied entirely upon traditional craft skills and natural materials as an alternative to the factory-produced goods spewing out of Victorian factories, all thin veneers of exotic woods and harsh textiles lurid with chemical color. In 1883, Morris met the young Ernest Gimson. At the time, Gimson was articled to a Leicester architect, but he was strongly attracted by Morris's theories of the decorative arts. In 1866, with the great man as mentor, Gimson went to London to study with the architect J. D. Sedding, who was a friend of William Morris.

At Sedding's studio, Gimson met Ernest Barnsley, and later Ernest's brother Sidney, the pupil of another notable architect, Richard Norman Shaw. Gimson and Sidney set up practice in an office around the corner from another young architect, Edwin Lutyens. But while Lutyens became an enormously successful architect on an international scale, Gimson and the Barnsley brothers struck off to the Cotswolds to establish a rural outpost of the Arts and Crafts Movement. They settled in the village of Sapperton. From there, they set about providing a completely integrated package of architecture, interior design, furnishings, and garden design, drawing on the skills of the local people and the materials and vernacular style of the region. This ethic of returning to the old-fashioned handcrafts and to the local vocabulary of architecture was a direct reaction to the uniformity and conformity engendered by the increasingly despised and slowly fading Victorian period, when the use of traditional materials and handcraft skills began fast disappearing in the face of expanding industrialization.

William Morris had recommended that Gimson study with Sedding, whose style embraced the Late Gothic and whose book, *Garden Craft Old and New,* had been published in 1891. It was followed in 1892 by *The Formal Garden in England,* written by Sir Reginald Blomfield. Both these works espoused a return to the formal style of the English Renaissance garden as being the one most appropriate for English houses and the only style that could be indentified as national.

They recommended that the garden be treated as an extension of the house and that layout be treated as rooms. They and their followers fervently believed that architecture had a place in the design of a natural space—not surprising, given their vocation and the current belief that the various arts should not be practiced in isolation.

In the preface to his book, Sedding wrote:

> Following upon the original lines of the Essay on the For and Against of Modern Gardening, I became the more confirmed as to the general rightness of the old ways of applying Art, and of interpreting Nature the more I studied old gardens and the point of view of their makers; until I now appear as advocate of old types of design, which, I am persuaded, are more consonant with the traditions of English life, and more suitable to an English homestead than some now in vogue.

In the text he describes how, near the house, there should be well-ordered terraces and "architectural accessories, all trim and fit and nice," then smooth lawns with a belt of fine trees, arranged with seemingly "divine carelessness," this then giving way to a "ferny heather-turf" and on into the distant woods. And it was the ability, he said, of the English garden of the Jacobean period (the gardens to which Sedding referred), to blend itself so artlessly into the natural surroundings that preserved it from any taint of artificiality. He also admired the Jacobean garden for its "air of scholarliness and courtliness: a flavour of dreamland, Arcadia and Italy."

Ultimately, it was the Italian ideal that inspired Sedding—in landscape and in architecture—for in the gardens and villas of Renaissance Italy he and Blomfield saw the original inspiration for the English ideal: "splendidly adorned, with straight terraces, marble statues, clipped ilexes and box, walks bordered with azalea and camellia, surrounded with groves of pines and cypresses, so frankly artistic, yet so subtly blending itself into the natural surroundings into the distant plain," is how Sedding described it.

John Dando Sedding's proposal for a formal garden in the English style, replete with topiary figures and a controlled axial view through the garden; gates frame the countryside scene, where trees are sited to continue the vista. From *Garden Craft Old and New*, 1891.

Blomfield's book was an essay on the history of the English garden reaching back to the Tudor gardens. With descriptions of early gardening literature and plants and their use, he explained how these early gardens were laid out, the correct use of architectural ornament in the garden, and other structural features that play a part in the successful composition of a "Formal Garden."

To both these men, the great landscape parks laid out in the eighteenth century by Capability Brown and his followers, who had swept away most "old-fashioned" (i.e., formal) English gardens, were nothing short of disasters. Equally, the bedded-out exotics flourishing in the parks and great gardens of Victorian England were anathema, mere displays of horticultural showmanship that deprived England's native flora and choice hardy perennials of their rightful place in the ornamental garden.

This last condition, the "bedding-out" commonly practiced by Victorian gardeners in private and public grounds, had also most grievously agitated William Robinson. He was an Irishman who had started out as an under-gardener at Glasnevin Botanic Garden, Dublin and ended up as the arbiter (to some) of what could and could not be considered good English garden taste.

Robinson had turned to publishing in the early 1860s and began his attack on the system of bedding-out tender, mostly annual, exotics in regimented beds in lines and blocks of garish color. He wrote *The Wild Garden,* published in 1870, in which he advised the "planting out of perfectly hardy exotic plants under conditions where they will thrive without further care." He wanted to see perennial plants grown in natural groupings that would require little or no attention.

When Sedding's and Blomfield's works appeared praising formal gardens, Robinson thought they were advocating bedding-out designs and began his war of words. He was a man whose ego thrived on contention. But both his rivals were up to the fray, and the resulting rhetoric and lurid prose with which they defended their respective cases is a study in period literature. Thus was born what became known as the "Battle of the Styles."

Robinson maintained that it was the "stereotyped Italian or geometrical design" of gardens that led to geometrical [bedded-out] planting and that, confronted by such a layout, people were "afraid to be free or natural" and so planted in straight, unnatural lines. Furthermore, he despised the wasteful recurrent expense of raising tender exotics under glass to bed out for a garish short-lived show, and the ugliness of the garden once the withered plants were uprooted, since the beds were left naked until the following season.

Additionally, the Blomfield-Sedding formalists maintained that only "Artists" (architects, painters—those with a trained visual sense) should be responsible for the layout of a garden. Indeed, many of the gardens being made at that time were laid out by artists like the watercolorist Alfred Parsons, and we all know that Lutyens was an architect and Gertrude Jekyll by training a watercolorist. This stance greatly irritated Robinson, who held that only a gardener with a thorough knowledge of plants could properly plan a garden. He wrote, "Plans are essential for busy men in offices, but the man who would make the best of his ground can do better without any plan but such as he marks out on the ground himself."

The upshot of this was Robinson's *Garden Design and Architects' Gardens,* which he published in 1892 and in which he intended to undermine and devalue the theories and work of Blomfield and Sedding. Robinson's argument was focused on what he determined was the unnatural effect of a formal plan. However, he conceded, "Formality is often essential in the plan of a flower garden near the house—*never* as regards the arrangement of its flowers or shrubs. To array these in lines or rings or patterns can only be ugly wherever done." So it would seem that he was entirely against a formal plan, yet he thought that building houses on artificially terraced sites was wrong because only the natural lines of a site should be used and "improved" if need be—but never terraced. (When Johnston was creating the Theatre Lawn, he shifted tons of topsoil to level the site and create the dais around the beech trees. The spoil was then utilized to elevate the Stilt Garden and gazebos.)

Robinson continued in this vein, lamenting the use of high walls and hedges to contain the garden and describe its linear plan, since this would mean that the shrubs used for the hedging would have to be clipped into "unnatural shapes." Blomfield replied by adding a preface to the second edition of his book, and the heated exchange continued unabated.

In 1896, Gertrude Jekyll felt compelled to arbitrate and decreed that both sides had something worthwhile to contribute. She suggested that the formalists were wrong not to take advantage of the horticultural innovations that had been introduced since the mid-1800s and hinted that, while Robinson was to be admired for promoting the widespread use of exotic hardy plants, those plants could perhaps be better appreciated in a more formal setting than the "natural" one he advocated. Gertrude Jekyll was the leading gardening authority at the turn of the century. She wrote for and edited Robinson's publications and revolutionized the role of color in the garden, applying color theory as practiced by artists to the way in which flower color was used. She had studied with the watercolorist Hercules Brabazon Brabazon, and treated the tints of foliage and petal as a painter treats his pigments, manipulating the dynamics of color harmonies to achieve a desired pictorial effect.

Robinson grudgingly accepted that a modicum of formality near the house was permissible but continued his campaign against formal gardens until at least 1905, when in his journal *Flora and Sylva* he published a number of articles preaching against the trend to formalism, which, to his probable dismay, was becoming widely accepted.

Two years before Miss Jekyll's arbitration, a garden designer named Thomas H. Mawson had worked in partnership with the architect Ernest Newton on the design of a house called Red Court near Haslemere in Surrey. Around the house, he ranged a number of hedge-enclosed rooms, carpeted with lawns bordered by flower beds all in the most formally balanced layout and placed along a central axis. The formal beds near the house then dissolved gradually into a "natural" or "wild" landscape of shrubs and trees in the style of William Robinson. In this manner, Mawson drew together two supposedly disparate types of garden and created a unified and satisfying whole. Nevertheless, the parts comprising the whole maintained their clearly defined indentities as areas where either "art" or "nature" was in command.

Mawson was an established and influential designer; he had set up his own practice in the Lake District in 1885, at the age of twenty-four, and seven years later was winning medals for his work. In 1900, Mawson's book *The Art and Craft of Garden Making* was published, the title proclaiming his affiliation with the Arts and Crafts group.

The principle of Mawson's design was to link the house to its surrounding landscape by repeating the architectural qualities of the building in its immediate vicinity, and then gradually to assimilate the built landscape into the natural one, but only if "the character of the surroundings justify it." In his estimation, "the region of the former [the garden area nearest the house] is the domain of architectural gardening or garden architecture; the latter [the areas that extended into the natural terrain] landscape gardening so-called, or as our American friends designate the art, landscape architecture."

Mawson was writing at the time of the last great surge of country house–building, and his theories relate directly to an architect–garden designer partnership. In his opinion, the layout of the house was as relevant to the use and enjoyment of the garden as the layout of the garden was to the house, and this being so, the balance and function of the interior (house) rooms should relate to those of the exterior (garden) rooms.

He wrote that the ideal site for his ideal garden was one that commanded fine views, and one that had at least a gentle slope if it was not possible to build on a hillside. He devoted the garden area nearest the house to formal, balustraded terraces, the principal of which should be "approached from the house either from the conservatory or loggia at the southwest corner or the garden entrance from the drawing room." Mawson admired the use of vases, urns, and so on to ornament balustrades and walls, or else to have them arranged on terraces, simply marking the corners, or as gatepost finials.

Mawson also admired the use of topiary; the third edition of his book, published some thirty years after the first, features a page of patterns for topiary shapes. An illustration of a Mawson-designed hillside garden in an earlier edition features boxwood-edged beds divided by paths, the crossings of which are marked with topiary pillars of clipped yew and recalls nothing so much as the Pillar Garden at Hidcote. In fact, many passages in Mawson's book can be seen to relate directly to elements of the design of Hidcote and the gardens that belonged to Johnston's friends, including Newby Hall, St. Nicholas, and Abbotswood.

Mawson wrote that alpine and rock gardens should not be visible from the house, but any "natural dingle or depression which could be screened from the more important features of the grounds would form a fitting place for them." He quoted from a paper read at the Royal Institute of British Architects by its author, a Mr. Belcher: "In the art of laying out a garden, as in architectural design, there is a certain seductive mystery gained by partially concealing and judiciously screening some parts from the immediate view. By this means the imagination is tempted

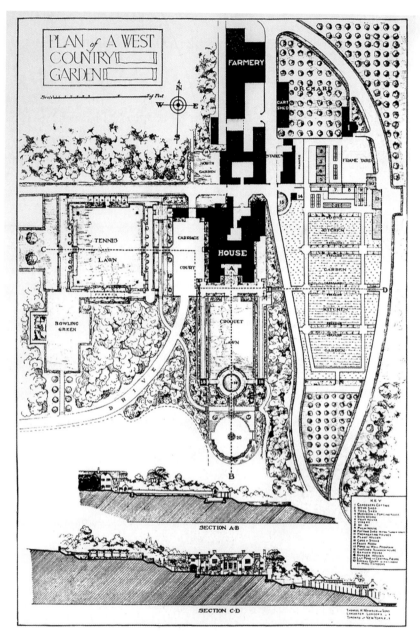

Mawson's plan for a terraced garden places the house at the center of the layout, with the garden rising and falling to either side with a cross-axial plan uniting the garden areas.
From *The Art and Craft of Garden Making*, 1900.

to conjecture the presence of hidden delights beyond and interest is quickened in expectation of some further enhancement." One of the great joys of Hidcote is the many little openings that beckon you on, leading you through hedges and down narrow paths to a seemingly never-ending revelation of beautifully composed garden pictures.

Mawson's interest did not end at the ground plan, but extended to the creation of the garden pictures framed by clipped hedges of holly, yew, and fern-leaved beech (*Fagus sylvatica* 'Asplenifolia'), which he favored. Mawson realized the importance of thoughtful planting. He advised the massing of plants in substantial groups: "Would that the faculty for mass-

Mallows's axial plan uses dense yew hedges to frame a long walk connecting the house to a terminal feature; in this case, a fountain surrounded by a pergola. From Gertrude Jekyll's *Gardens for Small Country Houses*, 1911.

ing was more prevalent, not alone in arranging the trees and shrubs but in the flower beds and borders also, instead of what is so prevalent; 'Everything by turns, but nothing long.'" He also determined it to be impossible to maintain all the garden borders in "fine display all year. Better to have areas of interest of successive display . . . February . . . snowdrops in the orchard . . . April . . . March . . . crocus in the lawns daffodils in the coppice," and so forth.

While all this will be familiar to readers of the first edition of this book, it is worth adding that Mawson brought together the ideas of his contemporaries as well as earlier practitioners, including Edward Kemp, the author of *How to Lay Out a Garden*, first published 1850. Kemp—who coined the phrase "a thing of beauty is a joy forever"—advised that "terraces, straight lines of walks, avenues of trees or shrubs . . . [and] all kinds of architectural ornaments will prevail" near the house, and in some cases throughout the garden. Though he admits that the formal style is expensive and requires considerable space to be well-displayed. In doing so, Mawson was instrumental in establishing a garden style that was eventually to become accepted as the norm. So much so that by 1914 it was described by Hermann Muthesius in *The English House* as being the quintessential English garden style, in which the garden began on a terrace near the house, and then proceeded to a transitional area of flower-bordered lawns through which the shrubberies and woodland areas on the perimeter were reached.

It is interesting to note that another architect and friend of Mawson, Charles Edward Mallows, had been designing in just this way for some time. He lectured to his Royal Academy students about the history of English gardens and was a recognized authority on the subject. Gertrude Jekyll was an admirer of his work, and had he not died suddenly, other architects (such as Mawson) might not have received so much attention.

Robinson may have lost the formalist argument, but his next book, *The English Flower Garden*, was responsible for initiating the trend of turning the garden into a plantsman's paradise. In it, he catalogued and described the cultivation in Britain of innumerable exotics that were flooding in from all parts of the Empire. These were the introductions of a new generation of plant-hunters, commissioned by the great botanical institutes or by private collectors, with a brief to discover material worthy of inclusion in the decorative garden, as opposed to greenhouse cultivation.

Another influential garden designer of the Edwardian period was Harold Peto (1854–1933). In 1876 he had set up in partnership with Ernest George (Edwin Lutyens was one of George's best students), with whom he stayed until 1892. Their partnership was dissolved that year, and Peto moved to the south of France, since he had agreed to George's request not to practice in England until 1907. Peto believed in delivering the complete design package, with the architect responsible for the interior décor and the garden layout and planting, as well as for the actual building. His architectural style was unashamedly derived from the villas and gardens of Renaissance Italy, and he had a natural talent for placing architectural ornament, statuary, pergolas, fountains, and so on in the garden scheme, so that what was essentially a classical Italian device for giving emphasis to a dramatic landscape worked equally well in a more restrained English setting.

Peto was also a knowledgeable and inspired plantsman with a profound understanding of the importance of form and color when applying plants to a design. In this, he was again displaying his affinity to the Italian ideal. He wrote:

> The entirely subordinate place in the [Italian] scheme that flowers occupy gives a breadth and quietude to the whole which is sympathetic, the picture being painted with hedges, canals and water tanks, broad walks with seats and statues and tall cypresses. If more of our English gardens could have an increase of this influence it would be well instead of their running riot in masses of colour irrespective of form. . . . It is difficult to understand what pleasure anyone can derive from the ordinary herbaceous border one sees without the slightest attempt at form, and the tall plants tied in a shapeless truss to a stake, and the most discordant colours huddled together.

Gertrude Jekyll was an admirer of Peto's work, and this, combined with his knowledge of plants, may have caused Robinson to think twice before condemning Peto's undeniably masterful use of architecture and the formal layout in a garden design.

Peto's exile in France was spent on the Riviera, where he designed the estates of wealthy Americans and European nobility, and the characteristics that identify these gardens as being Peto's work can be seen in the garden he created at Iford Manor in the shallow valley of the Frome near Bradford-on-Avon. The garden was a showcase for Peto's collection of Italian sculpture and ornament and also for the numerous plants he collected in the south of France. But while he valued the rarities, he preferred to use only those, usually common, plants of the correct form or color to create a scheme. He also worked on the design of Lord Redesdale's garden at Batsford Park, which is very near Hidcote and renowned for its collection of trees and shrubs.

Peto's gardens were typically devised as a system of terraces and garden rooms, each with its own theme, linked by long broad walks, marked where they crossed by circular or semicircular areas of lawn or paving. The walks terminated in either a garden house or pavilion, an arbor, a simple garden seat, or a spectacular view framed by an arcade or gateway. All these elements are evident at Hidcote.

Such was the architectural, intellectual, and artistic climate in which Lawrence Johnston began building his garden. Records at the Lindley Library of the Royal Horticultural Society show that Lawrence borrowed Mawson's book in 1904, Alicia Amherst's *History of Gardening in England* (1895), as well as Liberty Hyde Bailey's *Plant Breeding* (1897), Samuel Arnott's *The Book of Bulbs* (1901), and E. T. Cook's garden manual *Century Book of Gardening* (subtitled "a comprehensive work for every lover of the garden")—all before he had even owned Hidcote. Lawrence's mind was obviously on gardens, so it comes as no surprise that he borrowed Mawson's title, the most popular gardening book of the time.

In 1907, the year his mother acquired Hidcote, Lawrence borrowed Gertrude Jekyll's *Home and Garden* (1899) and *Wood and Garden* (1900); in 1910, W. Divers's book *Spring Flowers at Belvoir Castle* (1909) (the castle was the seat of the Dukes of Rutland presided over by Norah Lindsay's sister-in-law, Violet). Amherst's book clearly made an impression since Johnston borrowed it again in 1908 and in 1914. However, in 1915, while developing and designing the garden at Hidcote (it did not, after all, happen overnight), Lawrence personally borrowed Gertrude Jekyll's *Some English Gardens* (1904, with drawings by George S. Elgood), Sedding's *Garden Craft Old and New,* and H. Inigo Triggs's *Garden Craft in Europe* (1913). He also borrowed books about plants, greenhouse growing, and fruit tree cultivation. These lists, which cover roughly ten years, are the only ones the library has been able to locate but they do establish that Johnston read widely in the popular garden literature of the time and had a well-informed interest in old-fashioned English garden style. And with his finely tuned artistic awareness, and an untutored and therefore unprejudiced approach to the art of garden-making, he was able to absorb and draw together the various strands of each theory, resolving the arguments and creating a garden in which the disciplines of formal design and natural planting were united with the artist's use of form and color to shape a unique garden. Many years later, in a letter to James Lees-Milne, Johnston described Hidcote as a "wild garden in a formal setting."

The chronology of the garden begins naturally enough in 1907 with the laying-out of the area described as the Old Garden. Taking the cedar of Lebanon as his starting point, Johnston planned a long walk stretching west that terminated where the twin gazebos now stand.

Around the cedar and in closest proximity to the house, he created the enclosure known then as the Phlox Garden, but now called the White Garden, which came directly off the southern edge of the Cedar Lawn. In the corner created by it and the lawn, he made the Maple Garden. Both these gardens have small boxwood-edged beds, and in the White Garden there was a circle of lawn, since paved, on which a sundial was centered. The path from here into the Maple Garden runs centrally between two oblong beds and terminates at a bench surrounded by raised beds made with brick retaining walls. Plants in wooden tubs and terra-cotta urns lined the low walls, giving vertical interest.

To the west of these areas, the remaining space is marked into rectangular beds divided by secondary paths running parallel to the main one leading from the cedar. This part of the garden, with its topiary embellishments, small boxwood-edged beds, and pots of plants, has a marked medieval character.

Passing through the gates from the Old Garden, one enters what is known today as The Circle, a simple round of grass that marks the crossing axis of the path that leads into the Bathing Pool Garden. This sequence is a superbly thought-out use of the space. The previous area is composed entirely of squares and rectangles, but now circles dominate the ground. The anteroom above the Bathing Pool is composed of circular paths set within two squares, their corners taken up by boxwood-

A recent photograph of the main axis leading from the Cedar Lawn, past the twin gazebos, to the gate-framed view of the surrounding countryside, 2008. NPTL/Andrew Lawson

Looking along the perennial borders toward the twin gazebos. Note the immature stilt hedge and gate piers that now hold elaborate wrought-iron gates framing the view across the Vale of Evesham, c. 1910–15.

edged beds. The circular Bathing Pool, set below the anteroom terrace, was originally surrounded by wedge-shaped beds, and a convex curved stairway led out of the pool into another circular enclosure of unadorned lawns surrounded by hedge.

The White Garden and the Bathing Pool Garden entrance were, even then, planted with well-grown topiary specimens, which in Johnston's day were easily purchased from specialist nurseries, ready-trained and sizable enough to make an instant contribution to the garden.

Trelliswork was used in addition to the hedges to divide the garden area into separate rooms, sometimes as a temporary measure until such time as the hedges were fully grown, in other cases simply to provide an alternative, for Johnston no doubt realized that endless miles of hedging could become monotonous. This understanding may have been what inspired him to create the tapestry hedges of copper and green beech, box, holly, and yew for which Hidcote is famous.

These early parts of the garden are laid out within the old brick walls of the original garden area of the manor house; Johnston was fortunate

The White Garden at midsummer, 2008; the topiary and box hedges are painstakingly maintained in their original form, but planting schemes here and in other parts of the garden may be altered from time to time to reflect the changing nature of the garden in Johnston's era as his plant interests diversified and his gardening expertise increased. Andrea Jones to have the mellow old walls to lend some initial structure to his plan. In the remaining areas, created in the field beyond the walls, Johnston improved the natural terrain, which inclined toward the south, to create the series of terraces that comprise the Bathing Pool Garden.

A stream that crosses the garden northeast to southwest feeds the Bathing Pool, creating a shallow dell. Mrs. Winthrop's Garden is set above this dell and commands a superb southerly view. This little space was originally set quite apart from the other parts of the early garden and was intended to recall the gardens of the Riviera, where Gertrude had spent so many years. Sheltered by hedges and with an open aspect to the south, it is a perfect sun-trap, vibrant with blue and yellow flowers. These were her favorite colors and the planting today reflects that preference.

Passageways clipped in the yew hedge frame interior views leading to other areas of the garden, 2007. Andrew Lawson

During the summer, feather cushions in blue and yellow covers were scattered on the low brick steps edging the circular platform that forms the centerpiece of the garden. Terra-cotta tubs of standard lemon verbena stood on the brick pedestals.

To further the theme of color areas, the double borders edging the long grass walk that forms the main axis of the garden were planted to be predominantly scarlet; in the early days this area was referred to as the "Scarlet Borders," (now called the Red Borders) and each border had repeat plantings of pampas grass along its length. Parallel to and running along the northern edge of the Red Borders, Johnston and his team of garden hands began work on the area that later became the Theatre Lawn.

Work on the garden slowed with the outbreak of the First World War, when not only the Major but many of the men of the hamlet went to war, leaving only a few hands to maintain what had thus far been established. However, in 1915, and presumably while the Major was back at Hidcote recovering from his injuries (and reading Sedding's and Triggs's books), the Stilt Garden was planted on a terrace above and extending from the walk between the Red Borders. The change of level was marked by twin gazebos constructed to either side of a flight of stone stairs. The walk finishes at a double gateway that frames the view over the Vale of Evesham. At this point, the land drops away sufficiently to create the impression that the boundary of the garden is at the edge of the world.

When attempting to understand any garden, it is worth considering what was or may have been the main entrance to it. The relevance of this is best understood at the gardens of the Villa d'Este at Tivoli. Today the garden is entered from the villa on the uppermost terrace. It has been suggested that this is backward, and that originally the garden was approached from the bottom terrace. This makes a great deal more sense, since from the lower entrance, one progresses through a series of terraces, each more impressive than the last, with the music of the numerous fountains increasing in volume proportionately, from a single splashing jet to the fabulous water organ, until one reaches the villa, resplendent at the summit. Taken in reverse, the final effect is almost a letdown, like having the wedding cake first and finishing with the peanuts.

At Hidcote, Johnston brought his guests into the garden from the

Early views, c. 1910, of the garden areas that open off the main axis from the Cedar Lawn to the gazebos; note the smaller pool and the pie-shaped beds surrounding it. Seymour Preston

View to the Bathing Pool Garden, 1988. The geometry of clipped hedges and topiary define the interior spaces and, as photographer Andrew Lawson once observed, hint at Johnston's awareness of modernist design. Andrew Lawson

best room of his house (as one of the earliest English writers on garden design, William Turner, c. 1617, recommends), or from the entrance court at its front, rather than from a corner of the rear, workaday court-yard, from where for many years the National Trust positioned it. This entrance led visitors past the kitchens and outbuildings in the farmyard and along a curving path and brought them into the center of the main avenue, at the rond-point of The Circle. At this point, three vistas were available, and a decision then had to be made on which direction to go, diminishing the dramatic emphasis of the allée stretching from the Cedar Lawn platform to the Stilt Garden platform. The garden's carefully executed plan was diluted and muddled.

Johnston entered his garden from the house, through the small door at the back of the manor, or alternatively through the small door to the left of the house entrance that led from the courtyard onto a small terrace on the west front of the house, and which, as described by Nancy Lancaster, was full of pelargoniums and scented leaf plants, planted out and in pots. Stretching away to the west from the front door of the house is a long vista terminating in a statue of Hercules. Passing across the terrace, you come directly onto the Cedar Lawn and the breathtaking view of the main axis of the garden.

This glorious vista leads you on, passing through the quiet cottagey planting of the Old Garden, where the flower colors are softly muted tints of pink, blue, and ivory. From there, you pass on to The Circle, where the predominant color, except when the lilacs flower in May, is green. You then proceed to the Red Borders, where the opulence of color and the luxuriant dramatic planting prepares you for the stately march of pleached trees that constitute the *palissade à l'italienne* of the Stilt Garden, finishing at the perfect view of distant hills and Evesham's gentle vale. As you progress along this main artery, the other parts of the garden are gradually revealed and can finally be understood to make a supremely satisfactory whole.

The garden rooms at Hidcote are often regarded as being highly original innovations. This, as is evident from Peto's work, is not the case. Likewise, at Rous Lench Court not many miles from Hidcote, the Reverend Chafy-Chafy began, in 1876, to create a garden of ten terraces on a west-facing slope. In the scheme, he incorporated the remains of a Restoration garden and divided the terraces into garden rooms with yew and boxwood hedges. Chafy-Chafy and his architect traveled to Italy to study the design of its great gardens and incorporated what they saw in the plan of Rous Lench. Within the rooms, he planted roses and flower borders and without, at the perimeter of the garden, he made a fine pinetum. In 1899, *Country Life* magazine declared that Rous Lench had "scarcely a peer in England." The most striking similarity, however, is found in the eighteenth-century so-called Dutch gardens at Westbury Court, Gloucestershire, where a long canal bordered on each side by a tightly clipped hedge terminates at a brick-built pavilion; translated into Hidcote terms, the water reads as the hedge-framed, grassy esplanade of the Long Walk terminating in the little gazebo raised on its platform. The Westbury garden was in a ruinous state when the National Trust

The manor house at Hidcote, clad in ivy, from a photo provided by Jack Percival, c. 1930. Note the plants curtaining the walls and framing the window openings. Ethne Clarke

The main entrance to Hidcote Manor was at the side of the house; Johnston converted the building on the left into a chapel. 1988. Ethne Clarke

The National Trust has recently restored the tiny parterre garden through which guests exit the manor house into the garden. 2008. Andrea Jones

Reinstating the entrance parterre and its pebble-edged pathways returned the axial focus leading from the manor to the statue of Hercules at the end of the lime avenue, 2008. Andrea Jones

began its restoration in 1971, but forty years earlier, its charms might have been less tarnished and capable of suggesting a dramatic vista to an adventurous garden-maker like Johnston.

Part of Johnston's achievement was to recognize the potential offered by the garden rooms and to see that they would provide the shelter necessary for growing difficult exotics. The traditional plants of the old-fashioned English garden upon which Johnston initially relied were gradually supplemented by the treasures he was becoming increasingly fond of collecting for his garden, and in this way he took the first steps toward what has become for many people the main reason for having a garden: the display of choice plants grown in situations to which they are best suited, and grown for their own sake rather than for the sake of the garden picture.

There was reputed to be a box of documents pertaining to the development of the gardens that was allegedly handed over to the National Trust by the auctioneers who handled the dispersal of the contents of Hidcote Manor after Johnston's death in 1958. While these documents have never come to light, a cache of appointment diaries was recovered, but they tell more about Johnston's social engagements than about his designing. However, the books—a notebook for the years 1925–28 and two engagement diaries for 1929 and 1932—open a small window on to Johnston's character, his friends and concerns. He was an observant man; he sketched a decorative bed hanging at Mount Stewart, Ireland, and, typical of gardeners throughout history, noted plants that caught his attention in Mount Stewart's remarkable garden and then recorded the address of a good nursery. He was practical; there's a recipe for pickling hams, and shopping lists to remind him to purchase garters as well as groceries, seasick tablets, and Listerine. He was well connected: the 1932 diary indicates that he took a trip to Italy and visited gardens; Lady Sybil Lubbock's address at Gli Scafari in Lerici is recorded. Lady Sybil was the ex-wife of Geoffrey Scott and an intimate friend of art connoisseur Bernard Berenson. Cecil Pinsent, who created I Tatti for Mary and Bernard Berenson, had built Gli Scafari, as well as La Foce, the villa and garden of Sybil's daughter Iris Origo, in the 1920s. And Johnston noted in his diary, "BBs love Madonna"—this may be a reference to the Berensons, who were collectively known as the BBs and perhaps shared Johnston's admiration

The remains of the Dutch-style, eighteenth-century water garden at Westbury Old Court were not far from Hidcote and may well have been familiar to Johnston, judging from the resemblance of this view of the yew to the return vista from the end of the Long Walk at Hidcote. NTPL/Derek Croucher

of a sculpture or painting of the Madonna. Johnston's garden book, described by Frank Adams's daughter and Jack Percival as a record of the plantings at Hidcote, vanished after his death. Therefore, any study of the evolution of the garden can only be constructed from the memories of those involved or who had some peripheral knowledge of the course of events.

Hidcote Manor Garden has repeatedly been likened to a collection of cottage gardens, and certainly if the Major had ended his scheme with the garden rooms clustered around the house, this would have been true. But we can see that his intentions were far more sophisticated by the setting-out of the long avenue that leads from the Lebanon cedar to the final view seen from the Stilt Garden.

Major Johnston was a well-traveled man. Having spent much of his youth in France, he would have had knowledge of the elegant gardens of the Loire châteaux and the staggering effects to be achieved by emphasizing the passage along an allée with a series of well-placed transitions. He may have visited the great Renaissance gardens of Italy when he had that period of leave in 1913 and discovered their makers' virtuosity at merging the garden into the landscape by bringing the distant view into the garden plan—he was certainly visiting them in the late 1920s and early 1930s.

Particularly in Tuscan gardens, it is the case that main garden elements are composed solely to emphasize the vista, usually of the city nearby; in the hillside gardens of Fiesole and Settignano above Florence, the Palazzo della Signoria and the Duomo are the focus, or, as in the case of the fortified Villa Celsa, distant Siena can be seen from the fountain terrace below the castle's façade. In this way, Johnston, whether he was aware of it or not, fulfilled the criteria set out in an Italian architectural treatise of the fifteenth century. Written by the architect Leon Battista Alberti, it advised a hillside site for villas and gardens, for the health-giving openness to sun and fresh air (remember Johnston's weak lungs) and the important views "that overlook the owner's land . . . a great plain and familiar hills and mountains," with a foreground frame composed from what Alberti termed a "delicacy of gardens."

As well as making a garden, Johnston enlarged the manor, adding a wing to provide his own, separate accommodation. His section of the house encompassed the wing that is at right angles to the main block of the old manor house, and his apartment looked south over the garden, with the view unimpaired by the cedar of Lebanon. He also arranged for rainwater to be collected in a cistern in the "stone room," in the manor's attic. From there, water was piped to Johnston's bathroom, filtered and heated so that he could bathe in the soft, natural water.

At some point in his life, Johnston had converted to Catholicism. It has been said that this occurred during his youth in France, under the influence of a childhood tutor. Given Gertrude's Episcopal upbringing, it seems doubtful that any tutor would have lasted long had she discovered the spiritual corrupting of her cherished son. Nevertheless, whenever it occurred, it was another move that took him a step further from his mother's influence. So, in keeping with his desire to establish a fine estate, he entertained the idea of converting a stable building into a small chapel. Helped by his closest friend Reggie Cooper, he got only as far as putting in the windows and a chapel bell, and the space ultimately became a repository for odds and ends. His cousin, Elsie Mitchell, writing in May 1989, recalls that according to "Great Aunt D, the family member who knew cousin Lawrie best, he seemed to forget about his conversion to Catholicism at some point during World War II, [which] she attributed to a bomb

The lilac-framed gateway between the Old Garden and The Circle, 2008. The manor house fills the background. NTPL/Andrew Lawson

that exploded near him while he was an air raid warden." She continues: "The little chapel was probably never consecrated because of strenuous maternal objections. The family considered Lawrie's conversion *peculiar*. Since he may have become a Catholic for the same reason that he participated in the Boer War, maybe he simply became less interested in the religion after his mother's death . . . she was a formidable lady."

In the area now designated the Pine Garden, he had one of the farm outbuildings made into a plant house with a glass-fronted wall facing the Lily Pool; known as the Summer House, it was removed by the National Trust, but the pool remained. (Now rebuilt, the Trust calls it the Plant House.)

In 1921, Johnston further refined the sophistication of the garden by enlarging the Bathing Pool to its present size, so that it all but fills its small enclosure. In so doing, he got rid of the fussy collection of pie-slice-shaped flower beds and the clutter of paths. Functionally, he simply wanted a place for his friends and neighbors to swim (the daughters of the Muir family at Kiftsgate Court made frequent use of the pool), deepening one end so that swimmers could jump in. The adjacent thatched "Italian House" served as

The Bathing Pool began as a much smaller water feature, but was enlarged to provide outdoor entertainment for Johnston's friends and neighbors. 1998. Ethne Clarke

a changing room, and at other times Johnston and his guests would meet there for cocktails, seated on chairs and benches from Johnston's collection of Regency garden furniture; the little circular grass enclosure in the next garden room would have been an ideal spot for sunbathing.

Aesthetically, the transitions within this area are marked by the entirely different character of each space; positive areas are created by the geometric motifs of the boxwood-edged beds and the reflected pattern of clouds and foliage on the water's surface in the pool, and they contrast with the negative spaces of plain grass in the circles of lawn at the entrance and exit. This constant use of contrasts, positive and negative, mass and void, is carried throughout the garden and provides movement, so that one is constantly drawn from one place to the next and endlessly surprised by each new experience. It is difficult to be bored at Hidcote.

By 1922, work on the garden must have been consuming most of
Johnston's energies. He always thought of himself as his own head gardener, organizing the workforce and directing the landscaping. His horticultural knowledge would have increased enormously, as he was
reputed to have read many of the major gardening works of the time,
including plant monographs and the accounts of plant-hunting expeditions. His wide circle of friends was composed almost entirely of other
garden-lovers, and there can be no doubt that much of his expertise and
inspiration would have come from them. Anyone who moves in a gardening milieu will know of the cross-fertilization that occurs as plants
and ideas change hands. But, most importantly, experience is the best
teacher, and he would have had a great deal of that over fifteen years of
garden-making. The Major's plans, which came with great bursts of

This is the postcard "Pop" Brown, Johnston's valet, sent to his wife from the south of France; an X on the right edge
marks the location of Serre de la Madone, which Johnston purchased in 1924 to be near the sanitorium where
Gertrude was a patient.

enthusiasm, were often inspired by features he had encountered in other gardens he visited, both in England and abroad.

Johnston retained his association with France, and in the early 1920s he began to look for a suitable property. His mother and their butler, "Pop" Brown, accompanied him to the south, and they took a villa in the hills near Menton in the Val de Gorbio. Pop sent a postcard to his wife showing the Sanatorium de Gorbio, with the villa that Lawrence had purchased marked by Pop with an X. Its proximity to the Sanatorium influenced his choice; Gertrude suffered from aphasia, was becoming increasingly delusional, and had become a resident patient at the sanatorium. Johnston may also have felt the need for a milder climate: by this time he had only one lung. When and why he lost the other is not known, nor is it known when he contracted malaria, which was also affecting his health.

The south coastal regions of France had long been recognized as suitable for invalids, especially for consumptives, since tuberculosis was, until the 1930s, a usually fatal disease and widely spread through all classes and countries. In the early 1800s, doctors sent their wealthy patients to Nice, where the even climate and the mild and fragrant breezes were thought to help clear their lungs.

James Henry Bennet first recommended Menton as a health resort in 1859. He was an English doctor with a London practice and had himself been consumptive. During a winter spent in Menton, he discovered that the microclimate, created by surrounding mountain ranges that protect it from cold winds and the nearness of the sea, provided exactly the conditions necessary for a full recovery. Bennet's work was well known in the United States, and beginning in the 1860s, wealthy American families sent their weakened kin to Menton, hoping that their lungs would clear in the balmy Mediterranean climate.

Bennet recommended that his English patients should leave for France by the second week of October and return to England at least by the middle of May. This was to become Lawrence's pattern for his annual withdrawal to his Mediterranean villa. In January 1924, Lawrence purchased the first piece of land and the villa called Serre de la Madone; subsequently, in 1928, '30, '33, and '39, he increased his holdings by buying parcels of land from neighboring properties.

Now with a winter retreat in the south of France, the Major estab-

lished a routine that saw him in residence at Serre de la Madone from
September to March or April, when he would return to Hidcote in
time to enjoy the spring bulbs. Then, the following autumn, he would
once again move his household to Menton and the altogether milder
climate of the Mediterranean. The chauffeur, Fred Daniels, drove the
Bentley, and Johnston his sporty Lancia. Johnston had wanted Frank
Adams to go with him to Menton to begin the gardens there, but Mrs.
Adams was unwilling to make the move. Therefore, during Johnston's
winter absence, the Adams family lived in the manor as resident caretakers. A young gardener named Frensham, who had been trained by
Lawrence's friend the Hon. Robert James in his Yorkshire garden, St.
Nicholas, was hired and moved with his family to the villa. (The climb-
ing roses 'Bobbie James' and 'St. Nicholas' commemorate this fine
plantsman and his garden.)

While the Major was gone, Frank Adams would put into operation
all the plans they had worked on during the summer at Hidcote. Each
Sunday when Lawrence was at Hidcote, the two men remained clois-
tered in Johnston's study, working out the next phase of the garden.
Johnston recognized Adams's ability and was inclined to respect his
opinion if, for example, Adams said that a scheme was not feasible (or
too expensive to consider). It seems to have been an ideal working partnership built on mutual respect for each other's abilities and acceptance
of each other's shortcomings. Johnston was the dreamer, Adams the
man of practicalities.

After the war, one of the first projects at Hidcote was the Pillar Garden, which was set out in 1923. Separated from Mrs. Winthrop's Garden
by a broad grassy strip that led down to the stream, it was a hedged
enclosure studded with conical topiary yews. The planting was predominantly of Mouton peonies, and the bank along the western boundary
beyond the Pillar Garden was planted entirely with irises. A rock garden
was sited nearby.

In 1926, the woodland area at Hidcote, known as Westonbirt, was
planted. The Major had been to visit the famous arboretum of that
name located at the southernmost end of the Vale of Gloucester. This
arboretum had been started in 1829 by Robert Holford and had one
of the finest collections of trees and shrubs in the country. Johnston
was so taken by what he saw there that he returned with Adams to

show him the effect he wished to create in the new area of garden he was planning.

By this time, Hidcote was recognized as being one of the premier English gardens, and many of the trees acquired for the scheme came from Westonbirt Arboretum, given to Johnston by Lord Morley, who at that time owned Westonbirt and who was renowned for his generosity, distributing plants among the cognoscenti.

In the autumn, the color of the changing foliage in this new part of the garden was incremented by the resident flamingos, who stalked through the shrubberies and rested with the cranes in the pool that once was central to the layout of this area of woodland garden. The birds were rather curious additions to the native fauna, and quite a few were lost before Johnston and Adams thought to have the birds' wings clipped. Also resident in Westonbirt was, of all things, an ostrich.

Johnston's desire to collect the rare and unusual meant some radical alterations to the natural soil and drainage of the garden. Teams of men were employed to excavate parts of the garden so that an enormous tonnage of peat could be added to create areas with the high acidity needed to cultivate rhododendrons, azaleas, acers, and other calcifuge specimens.

The expense of these grandiose schemes brought Lawrence up against his mother's financial controls, which affected him even after her death (at Serre de la Madone on December 8, 1926). Gertrude's chief concern for Lawrence was his lack of any financial sense, and she arranged by the terms of her will that Lawrence would not be able to touch the capital of her estate, but would receive the income from $1,239,936, which, after his death, was to revert to the estate. Lawrence was aghast at this outcome, for it meant he would have no access to the capital and was thus subject to an allowance granted by his mother's trustees.

Lawrence must have had an inkling of future difficulties, for in August 1925 the English Courts of Protection granted an application brought by Johnston to have Gertrude "declared incompetent because of senility, which has led her to believe she is being persecuted by her maid." Although the transcripts of the proceedings have long since been destroyed, the General Order, dated August 11, 1925, refers to Gertrude as "The Patient" and made Johnston "The Receiver," responsible for Gertrude's English property, and it allows him access to her resources to pay for her "journey to and winter residence in France," and permits

Mr. and Mrs. Merrill, Johnston's butler and housekeeper, with Timmy the spaniel, c. 1925. Note Merrill's casual footwear.

Lawrence "the use and occupation rent free" of Hidcote Manor (for although Johnston was to all appearances the head of the household, his mother owned the property). The case was reported in the *New York Times* on March 14, 1926, when the United States Supreme Court appointed the Bank of New York and Trust Company sole committee to administer Gertrude's American property. This amounted to $1,899,024, in deposits, stocks, bonds, and property, plus an annual income of $71,447 from realty and investments.

Part of the estate was left to her niece, Katherine Waterbury, and while Johnston had the interest from the lion's share, he was incensed that his cousin should take part of what he considered rightfully and entirely his own.

Nevertheless, this pecuniary tussle did not encourage him to take a firm hold of his own money management. Now, instead of turning to

Gertrude, he relied on his secretary, Miss Marsden, to administer his finances. She would often enlist Frank Adams's help in curbing Lawrence's wilder extravagances in the garden. In addition to Miss Marsden, Johnston could rely on his cook-housekeeper, Mrs. Merrill, to keep things running smoothly. By all accounts, this calm, efficient woman administered Johnston's life, serving as the de facto lady of the manor. With her husband, who was the major's new butler, she welcomed guests, sometimes as many as twenty or thirty, for gracious dinners, seeing particularly to the needs of female visitors. Nor did financial worries upset Lawrence's plans for Hidcote, which carried on at the same scale as before.

Three

THE GARDENER'S WORLD

Lawrence Johnston was not gardening in a vacuum, and in making Hidcote he was, as gardeners always are, greatly influenced by the gardens and gardening activities of his friends and contemporaries. Chief among these is the garden at Sutton Courtenay Manor, Oxfordshire, and the home of his intimate friend Mrs. Norah Lindsay.

Born in 1873, Norah was the second of five children of the Honorable Edward Bourke, a younger son of the Irish peer Lord Mayo. But to understand Norah, it helps to know something about her mother, Emma (Emmie) Hatch, a "daughter of the Raj."

Educated in Brussels from the age of five, Emmie grew into a poised and beautiful young woman, although somewhat a coquette, all too aware of her charm, her talents, and the advantages of her birth. Following her marriage and return to England, Emmie became an accomplished social climber, developing friendships with all the best-connected people until she eventually captured the golden ring by becoming a favorite of Edward, Prince of Wales (later King Edward VII). She became, as he called her, his "Dear Little Friend."

Norah inherited her mother's looks and, as it developed, her gregarious personality. She also inherited her mother's skill at social networking, beginning with Emmie's coterie of well-connected friends and acquaintances. On August 1, 1895, Norah married Captain Harry Lindsay, a younger son in a large, landed family. Norah's marriage home, Sutton Courtenay, near Oxford, was given free and clear to Harry as a wedding gift by his cousin, Lord Wantage, who later gave Norah the then princely sum of £5,000 to be her personal wealth.

The Lindsays' home and its gardens were as rich, colorful, and full of character as Norah herself. As is evident from a photo essay in *Country Life*, the house was imbued with the character of Old England: faded tapestries hung on the walls; opulent Italian brocades draped across carved oak tables and benches; pewter dinnerware gleamed on dresser shelves. Harry Lindsay's position in the family line meant he had to make his own way in the world. The army had provided a career, but after his marriage he soon retired his commission and tried to make a go of antique-dealing and furniture restoration, working from Sutton Courtenay.

Sutton Courtenay was an ancient manor house, listed in the Domesday Book, and required considerable restoration to make it comfortable. Harry diligently set about the task of restoring beams, interior woodwork, and plasterwork, using one of the old barns as his workshop and toolshed, while Norah began work on the gardens. The couple were acolytes of the Arts and Crafts Movement, which, given Norah's early affinity for the Souls, is not surprising.

Harry's sister, Violet Lindsay, was a leading member of the Souls; her artistic talents, great beauty, and original approach to life epitomized the Soulful credo. Their father, Lord Crawford, encouraged her considerable artistic talent and sent her to Italy to study art, while he encouraged Harry in the decorative woodworking arts.

Violet was married to John Henry Manners, heir to the 7th Duke of Rutland (their daughter was Lady Diana Manners, later Diana Cooper). She became recognized as an aesthete and was one of Emmie's close friends. Subsequently, she and Norah became friendly, and Violet's sketches of nineteen-year-old Norah, executed in the best traditions of the Pre-Raphaelite Brotherhood, reveal something of Norah's character as well as her beauty: in these sketches Norah glances up coyly from beneath heavy-lidded eyes; a froth of curls defines her forehead, while her oval face, pointed chin, and Grecian profile display the ideal beauty of the time. Norah was undeniably an enchanting young woman.

As Norah and Harry Lindsay restored the old Manor House, they soon found their own lives restored by the arrival of two children: Nancy, born barely a year after their marriage, and Peter, born in 1900. But then as now, the costs of renovation, added to the needs of a young family, put a strain on the Lindsay resources. Sutton Courtenay was a beautiful, historic, money pit—added to which were Norah's extravagant entertainments. Oxford male undergraduates were favorite guests (often they were the sons of her Soul friends), and the couple's frequent journeys to Italy and other European countries took their toll. Increasingly, the couple lived separate lives. At one point, when finances were particularly pinched, Norah told her younger sister Madeline (with whom she most often sought refuge from her problems) that she was determined to leave England for Italy to run a resort in an old Italian villa.

Norah and Harry Lindsay at the entrance to Sutton Courtenay Manor. From *Country Life*, 1904.

Things came to a head when Harry resumed his army career and returned to active duty. By 1905, Norah was, for all intents and purposes, alone but for her children. Still, she carried on her gay whirl of socializing and travel, as though indifferent or untroubled by her parlous state. Sutton Courtenay remained a financial drain, but the garden was her comfort and joy—and the foundation of her future income.

Norah's talents as a garden-maker were recognized early on, and the gardens at Sutton Courtenay were featured in a 1904 edition of *Country Life*. In styling her garden, Norah had adhered to the principle of relating the period of the garden to that of the house. There were three areas: the Long Garden, made in an enclosure of high brick walls and clipped box hedges, was planted with masses of old shrub roses, herbaceous borders, hedges of lavender and rosemary, around well-tended lawns and shady pergolas. Ponds, urns, and fanciful topiary work were dotted throughout the boxwood-edged beds, and woolly grey mullein towered overhead, self-sown on the top of the brick wall. Norah's plan in the Long Garden may have been formal, but the planting was luxuriantly informal.

The Pleasaunce and Wilderness lay next to the Long Garden. The Pleasaunce, created in an old orchard, was carpeted in spring with naturalized daffodils, crocuses, and narcissi, and in summer perfumed by more old roses and flowering shrubs of many types, including broom and gorse. This shrubby area gave on to the Wilderness, planted with deciduous trees.

The final area of the garden was known as the River Garden, for the river Thames was only about two hundred yards from the main garden. Here, in the damp grassy area along its bank, Norah planted moisture-loving shrubs, a walk of climbing roses, and an avenue of pleached limes that created a vista toward the water meadows and river beyond. She made a water-lily path that ran down the center of the rose walk: "A long redbrick path, bordered by grass, extends for 100 yards or so; in the brick path are sunk tanks of water, in which various colored miniature water lilies live, while overhead is a wooden pergola of climbing roses, the effect being very pretty" is how the garden was described in *Country Life* in 1904.

Norah used water to unite the various parts of her garden, a device widely used in the gardens of Italy, of which she was a great admirer. In 1931, Norah provided *Country Life* with another description:

> Indeed, there is more than a memory of Italy in my garden. . . . I would have been a much lesser gardener had I not worshipped at the crumbling shrines of the ancient garden gods of Florence and Rome. There I teamed the magic of black sentinel cypresses, translated in our northern clime to Irish yew and juniper—a severe architectural note, but mollified by the invariable vicinity of water. . . . All the walks of Sutton Courtenay end in pools or fountains with nearby seats to enjoy the different musics.

It is hard to pinpoint exactly when Lawrence Johnston and Norah Lindsay first met. Her biographer, Allyson Hayward, suggested that it was sometime in the early 1920s, judging by the first appearance of Johnston's name in Norah's correspondence at the time. However, James Platt, a botanizing and gardening friend of Nancy Lindsay, recalled meeting "an old lady, well over 95," who with her husband had been friends with Lawrence Johnston when *he first acquired* Hidcote. As Platt recounted, "they were able to see [Johnston] make the layout of the garden and watch the plants grow. She said whenever they went [to Hidcote], Norah was always there and that Nancy was usually with her."

Yet, somehow, it hardly matters, since Lawrence and Norah became the closest of friends, establishing a bond that lasted their lifetimes. Both understood the importance of consulting the genius of the place when creating their gardens. In Norah's case, the garden was made on a flat riverbank. Lacking the dramatic views with which Hidcote was so richly endowed and which Johnston so successfully exploited, she used water to end the walks and avenues, thereby bringing the natural landscape into the garden environs.

In Norah, Lawrence had found someone to complement his abilities and personality. Where he was shy and retiring, preferring to associate only with a select group of garden-lovers, Norah was ebullient and untiring in her devotion to her many and varied friends, who came from every age group. Nancy Lancaster recalls, "Norah had a light touch and children and old people were all her friends." Norah, like her mother Emmie, was a gifted musician and artist, and was wonderfully entertaining, as she had an original and ready sense of humor. This made her welcome wherever she went as a houseguest, for though genuinely loved by her friends, Norah was more than able "to sing for her supper," which became a distinct advantage when she later had to depend on those very same friends for financial support.

In her garden-making, from the earliest days, Norah liked formal layouts and informal planting, and used rather common flowers in large groups, like valerian and *Campanula latifolia* with red shrub roses. Her herbaceous borders were carefully color-schemed and planted in huge blocks. Studying her accomplishments, it is clear that Johnston, in his work at Hidcote, had been influenced not only by the trends of the day, but also by Norah as she adopted and shaped these trends to her own style—Norah had already achieved recognition as a talented garden designer before Johnston had even acquired Hidcote.

But the exchange was not one-sided. Norah's treatments were initially rather full—even overgrown—as can be seen in the photograph of her own garden at Sutton Courtenay, while Johnston, even in the first days of the Old Garden, demonstrated a more conservative restraint. Looking ahead, however, the friends seemed to switch tastes, as in later years, when Johnston had developed his garden in the south of France, Norah complained that the plan there was nonexistent: "There's no design, it's too tricky about with tiny paths and tiny rocks and tiny sitting places"; "[it's] certainly full of lovely individual plants, but one thing counteracts another—it's not planned." This from the woman who was loath to pull a seedling from a path and embraced topiary with the devotion of a zealot.

But their friendship was inviolable. Norah recognized Johnston as a "cosy companionable creature" who shared her "three passions . . . gardening, travelling and reading out [loud]. "He is," she wrote, "a good little man—that's why I like him." But she also likened him to Rumpelstiltskin—an ugly little gnome who demanded a woman's firstborn for teaching her to spin straw into gold!

There was one other area in which Lawrence Johnston substantially made his mark on their relationship. Nancy Lindsay, it would seem, Norah's firstborn, came to be regarded by Johnston as the child he never had. Of the many rumors drifting around about Nancy during her lifetime, perhaps encouraged by her colorful past, was one that she was, in

Nancy Lindsay as a young woman, c. 1922.

fact, Johnston's daughter. According to James Platt, there was a "supposition among Johnnie J.'s friends . . . and I heard it elsewhere, that he was Nancy's father." But if Nancy's year of birth is believed, and allowances made for Norah's earliest associations with Johnston (and her sisterly regard for him), it is unlikely to be the case. Besides, as Platt says, the idea was firmly rejected by Nancy, who was proud of her ancient and distinguished Lindsay heritage.

Perhaps Johnston's concern for Nancy was engendered not only by his friendship with her mother, by also by his recognition of certain similarities between them. The Lindsay family were not close. Nancy's parents' marriage had ended in separation: after retiring from the army, Harry Lindsay lived in London and went to work for an interior design firm, while Norah was based at Sutton Courtenay. Nancy had no formal schooling and her childhood was lonely and turbulent; just as Lawrence was smothered by his mother's devotion, Nancy's "talented and beautiful mother," as she referred to Norah, overwhelmed her. She seemed to be casting about in the wake of her popular and vivacious mother for a scrap of recognition, yet was always trying to disassociate herself from her parent. Nancy never liked to introduce her friends to Norah for fear they would transfer their affections to the older woman. In an effort to attract attention, Nancy was forever flying in the face of social convention, which only alienated strangers and made her a trial to her friends. Her cousin, the great society beauty Lady Diana Cooper, remembered that Nancy could "empty a ballroom in fifteen minutes," and Lady Diana's son, John Julius, Lord Norwich, said that in the family it was believed Nancy had been a prostitute in Germany between the world wars. One can't help but wonder if perhaps Lord Norwich was being a bit hyperbolic, since that generation of young women behaved and gloried in their liberated ideals of love and living for the moment. World War I had taken a terrible toll on Nancy's generation. The young people who remained were morally and emotionally numbed by the carnage and its aftermath, and many felt there was little to answer for and even less to live for. It was also suggested to me by several sources in the course of my research that the reason for Norah and Harry's separation had to do with his abuse of Nancy and Peter . . . something about his photography not being entirely whole-some. If this were true, it could explain Nancy's eccentricity. To her sister, Norah expressed her sorrow that Harry no longer loved her, and gave that as the reason for the breakup of her marriage. But it's hard to imagine that she would have revealed a less palatable truth. When asked, Norah's biographer suggested that Nancy herself might have been the source of this scurrilous rumor because she so disliked him, but also said that Nancy was on cordial terms with him and visited him often at his London home. What is certain from this stew of innuendo and rumor is that Norah and Nancy were each in their own way controversial individuals and that each had her own highly developed sense of personal drama.

At Hidcote, Nancy found a bolthole, especially useful when Norah was at home at Sutton Courtenay—Nancy would scurry to Hidcote to escape her. In the gardens at Hidcote, she also found an occupation to which she could devote her energies and which would occupy her solitary hours. Nancy had inherited some of her mother's talent for observation; her father had also pursued a hobby that required hours of patient study, for he was a keen ornithologist, and part of the garden at Sutton Courtenay had been a bird sanctuary (birds were a vogue garden accessory, it seems: Johnston had an aviary at Hidcote as well as one at Serre de la Madone).

Through a process of careful self-education, Nancy became a competent, if not accomplished, plantswoman. Her concerns were not her mother's or Johnston's, for she was only mildly interested in the way a garden was designed. She loved plants and, in the 1920s and early '30s, ventured off on plant-hunting expeditions around Europe, to Turkistan and the remoter parts of the Near East, most often traveling alone, as she determined that if she traveled with a man they would both almost certainly have been killed, while a solitary woman was safe. Nancy's most significant plant-hunting trip was the one she undertook in 1935 with Alice "Ozzie" Fullerton, who wrote about the trip in *To Persia for Flowers* (published in 1938 by Oxford University Press). Fullerton was well-connected to the British delegation in Iran and therefore useful to Nancy; she ensured that they were able to travel comfortably and without much difficulty. A year later, in 1936, Nancy received thanks from the Natural History department of the British Museum (where the Keeper of Plants, Captain Ramsbottom, was a friend), for the 430 plants she had presented to the Museum, which were "well preserved and [. . .] accompanied by full notes and several paintings." In the same meeting when this letter of thanks was dictated, Ramsbottom explained that Nancy proposed to go again later that year (1936) to "Meshet and to the north east frontier, and to collect for the Departments of Botany and Entomology." For this a grant of £25.0.0 was approved. In 1937, the Keeper reported that Nancy had collected 816 "numbers" or specimens, mainly in the provinces of Gilan and Yehlah near the Caspian Sea. She also included insects among her finds. Again, it was noted that "the plants are well preserved" and that they came from an area previously not represented in the department.

For this expedition Nancy kept track of her expenses and received, after some discussion, reimbursement for shipping costs. Her letters to Ramsbottom invariably conveyed some complaint, usually about how put upon she felt by the whole operation (it was costing her money she did not have, the specimen boxes the museum provided were too cumbersome and cost too much to ship, and so on).

Her notebooks and diaries (which I had with the first edition and later passed to her nephew David Lindsay, their rightful owner, but was unable to see again for this edition) revealed that she went to Sultanabad, now called Arak, southwest of the holy city of Qom in northern Iran, and contained numbered lists that may have refered to plant specimens she gathered: "22. Grass leaved gagea—Teheran golf course; 170. Moon-light cheiranthus; 283. Fringed carpet pink; 401. Fringed crysanthemu-mish comp [compositae?]: from Ashnastan [*sic*] cornfields." She traveled to Persia again in 1939, evidently with some support from Kew; in a let-ter to the curator she mentions a book she planned to write—if she could find the time.

Nancy, according to James Platt, referred to her ownership of plants as in "my colchicum from Persia." She was, he remembered, a "real eccentric in speech and sometimes in her actions," labeling a rose she found in the Elburz Mountains as an introduction by Alexander the Great's soldiers, or another rose found by the Caspian Sea as having arrived there in the load of a Silk Road caravan, even though such asser-tions were preposterous.

But Nancy's diary is not devoted entirely to plants. There are lists of the birds she spotted: "the two russet, black and white birds who made a melodious note like a reedpipe undulating [ululating?]"; the people she met, "Musayef like a gourd dancing the hulahula"; and events, "Fri 7, Scorpion fell on me." Most intriguing are the pages of adjectives divided into categories of color (henna, topaze [*sic*], bronze, olive dun) and con-trasts (moonlight and halflight, sunlight and shadow), textures, and so on (weather-gnawn rocks, congerie of peaks), as though she was flexing her syntax for a travel article or poem: "The air glittered, the pale-green and rusty fawn mountains were dappled with velvet-black shadows as we drove past a sand-dune tufted with fat little bushes of the cream (daphne) a pair of adolescent eagles orange and black and cream—cream rufts played leap-frog over the drosky."

A visit today to the Herbarium of the Natural History Museum in London, to view what could be found of Nancy's specimens and read through her labels, tells the story of a determined woman striking out in an area of study that was at the time typically the purview of men; going to a little-visited and often-dangerous region, with few resources other than her own grit (and often gall) to get her through. Perhaps this explains Nancy's thoroughness; many of the tiny three-inch by four-inch labels read like her later nursury catalog descriptions:

No. 692. Magnolia grandiflora var: Forms a great tree, commonly culti-vated, apparently from Time "immemorial" as there are great trees in some of the Pahlur Gardens. Most of the plants cultivated in Guilan and Mazan-deran from ancient times are reputed to come from Russia . . . "

No. 1000. Rosa centifolia var: of the three varieties of Rosa centifolia culti-vated in Lahijan this is the rarest being only found in two fields. The flow-ers are very large for a single rose, of a dazzling clear cherry. All three varieties have a strong perfume. They are grown extensively for rose-water, the petals pressed into a sticky cake and are also sold in the bazaars as a sweetmeat. All set seed; the oval hips are of a smooth bright orange. June.

No. 687 Jasminum. Climber. Differs from Jasminum officinalis in having smaller blunter leaflets, large panicles with larger flowers with red-infused reverse and scarlet buds. Jasminum officinalis is common both wild in the foothills and cultivated in gardens all over Guilan and the two are readily distinguished by their foliage. 687 is reputed to be of a more delicate con-stitution that Jasminum officinalis. Cultivated Guilan.

Reading this last label brings to mind the remark in Fullerton's book that one of the places Nancy sent live specimens was Menton, France; it is not unreasonable to suppose that she was sending them to Johnston at Serre de la Madone. Among the plants that Johnston is credited with introducing is a fine form of jasmine, *J. polyanthum*.

Nancy researched the local uses of plants, too, and on her labels included more ethnobotanical information than is usual. Even by today's standards, her work, as described by the current curator of the Herbarium, is important, and relevant to our understanding of that region's flora. In the mid-1990s, Nancy's surviving specimens were sent to Vienna and used in the preparation of the multi-volume *Flora Iran-ica*. In this way, the result of Nancy's garden work differs from that of her mother. Norah engaged (and in some instances exploited) her wealthy social connections by designing attractive gardens for them in order to support herself, while Nancy pursued a more lonely path with her plant-hunting work and nursery. She held her plants close; Rose-mary Verey recalled that Nancy had to approve of you before parting with anything from her nursery. Where Norah was compelled by her poor finances to flit from stately home to royal palace, Nancy in later years lived on the edge of social acceptance, chain-smoking Turkish cigarettes in her tumbledown cottage on the perimeter of her mother's former home.

Yet whether she would have cared to admit it or not, Nancy shared her mother's love of words, and Norah was noted for her gift of description. Nancy Lancaster, describing some of Norah's flights of fancy, recalled as a particular favorite her description of a mutual female acquaintance having "eyelashes like marabou." Norah's description of her garden at Sutton Courtenay in the 1931 *Country Life* article is enormously evocative: "Every garden should be a continuation of the house it surrounds, and where the dwelling is old and sleepy the garden, too, must be drowsy and lie under the spell of the ages, so that you are conscious of the years that have given the grey stone walls their gold and the heavy yew their girth."

Lawrence Johnston helped to inspire Nancy's preoccupation with plants, since she shared his desire to always have the best, in form, color, or scent; this was what, in her opinion, made a plant garden worthy. Johnston, in fact, was not quite so rigorous in his criteria and was willing to admit a suspect plant if it served a design purpose. And it may well have been Johnston who encouraged Nancy to undertake her plant-hunting expeditions, since this was something in which he was himself interested, offering as it did a way to increase the variety of rare and unusual plants in his gardens and, as we'll see later, to satisfy the "plant nerd" in him.

Norah gardened with as much panache as she lived her life, and her abilities as a garden designer provided a source of income when she found herself hard up in the years after the First World War. Norah traveled the length and breadth of Britain, with forays onto the Continent, to visit her garden projects commissioned by friends and associates. Apart from her fees, clients paid Norah an annual retainer to visit the gardens she designed, to keep a check on their progress (but these clients were also her friends and, as Norah's financial state worsened in time, the fee was one way they could help support her without the appearance of charity). Nancy Lancaster recounted how one had to be careful walking with Norah through a garden, for if she proffered any advice, one received a bill along with the bread-and-butter letter. One person she never billed, however, was Lawrence Johnston.

Her earliest paid commissions came just before 1914, from Lady Astor, who had Norah design the double borders at the entrance to

Cliveden, to be ablaze for Ascot Week. Later at Cliveden she rearranged the Long Garden, planted masses of camellias, and conceived the hillside planting.

In 1915, Harold Nicolson and Vita Sackville-West acquired Long Barn, near Sevenoaks in Kent. There they began work on what was to be the second of their three gardens, and consulted Norah about its plan. Thus, in their apprentice days, Vita and Harold were influenced by many of the same garden design principles as Lawrence Johnston. This early exposure to the use of garden rooms later informed the plan of Sissinghurst.

Later, at Kelmarsh Hall, the Northamptonshire home of Nancy Lancaster (Lady Astor's neice), Norah planned the border and opened up the yew hedges that surrounded the walled garden and planted masses of bulbs beneath the oak walk.

One of her best-known commissions was the restyling of the formal gardens at Blickling Hall, carried out in 1930. She did away with the inordinately fussy beds laid out all over the east lawn, which had been designed by William Nesfield, and retained only the four largest corner beds and their topiary cones, topiary that looks remarkably like squat versions of the yews in the Pillar Garden at Hidcote, which in turn recall the towering topiary cones that marched through the borders of Norah's own garden of Sutton Courtenay.

The beds are filled with herbaceous plants, those nearest the house in soft shades of pink, mauve, grey, and blue, with hot colors confined to the furthermost beds. The broad grass avenue, extending from the steps that lead up from the floral borders, terminates at the Temple. This plain grass sward is bordered by masses of shrubs planted beneath the tree canopy at the lawn edge. In spring, the Temple is buffeted by clouds of azaleas in shades of yellow, salmon, peach, and cream, making what is surely one of the finest sights in any garden today. This stunning effect is achieved with the simplest plan possible.

Norah never lost her affection for the old-world garden style, and at Blickling Hall she made an enchanting secret garden in a small opening in the woods to the side of the Temple avenue: two small rooms etched into the forest, one housing nothing more than a bench and sundial on a square of lawn, the other planted with lilies and scented shrubs, call to mind the *giardini segreti* of the Medici villas outside Florence.

Sir Geoffrey Jellicoe recalled that Norah was present on the occasion when he showed the garden plans he had devised to Mrs. Gilbert Russell, who then owned Mottisfont Abbey. In particular was a sketch for a parterre in front of the house; Norah said she knew just the historic pattern to fit the shape and pulled out a book showing it. The pattern, it transpired, loosely resembled the pattern of the transom above the door leading into the area of the parterre, so in that way Norah consciously or unconsciously followed the seventeenth-century tradition of using strapwork patterns in plaster pargetting and wood trims of old manor houses to design knots.

Other clients included the Eden family, whose garden overlooked the Venetian lagoon, and Edward, Prince of Wales, for whom she designed the gardens at Fort Belvedere and who drew considerable inspiration from her work. It was probably Norah who sent the prince to view the gardens at Hidcote Manor; he arrived one day accompanied by Mrs. Simpson, unannounced and unceremoniously, ready to pay his shilling with the others coming to view Hidcote on one of the days when the garden was open for charity.

While Norah Lindsay may have been Johnston's closest female gardening companion, as Hidcote grew and his recognition as a plant connoisseur advanced, Johnston entered the rarefied world of the Garden Society, all of whose members (limited to fifty at any one time) were Fellows of the Royal Horticultural Society and all men (women were not admitted) who had notable gardens and also focused their attention on cultivating, propagating, and exchanging new plant introductions. To acquire these plants, members participated in expeditions or else helped to fund them as subscribers, in exchange for which they received seed of plants brought back by the expedition to which they subscribed. Hidcote was known as a notable garden, and Johnston's skill with plants was equally admired. Introduced to the Society by Mark Fenwick, Johnston's neighbor at Abbotswood, he was a shoo-in and elected in 1922. The acquisition of Serre de la Madone simply consolidated his position, with two very different gardens in two widely dissimilar climates. Johnston had a need—and an eye—for many sorts of plants.

His plant-hunting began gently, with a trip in 1922 to the Swiss Alps in the company of the great alpine plantsman E. A. Bowles. From then on, Johnston took part in many botanizing forays to gardens all over

Britain and Europe, keeping a careful accounting of his expenses for each trip. Until her death in 1926, Gertrude kept a tight rein on her son's spending, but after that, with his inherited income at his disposal, Johnston's plant-hunting became more intense. He sponsored Frank Kingdon-Ward to Burma in 1926, and in 1927, Johnston himself took part in an expedition to South Africa. Led by Collingwood "Cherry" Ingram, the trip included, besides Johnston, his friend Reginald Cory, and Cory financed the participation of the young George Taylor (later the director of the Royal Botanic Gardens, Kew). The trip lasted four months and took the participants from the Drakensberg Mountains in South Africa to Lake Victoria and Mount Kilimanjaro in Tanganyika (now Tanzania). Taylor had graduated the previous year from Edinburgh and it was his first expedition. While he and Ingram collected quite a lot of material (his eventually went to Dufferin Castle), Sir George explained that for Cory the expedition was more of a "social affair" and he did not actively collect, and that Johnston did not scour the countryside as keenly as himself and Ingram, and in the field, at any rate, did not appear to be very knowledgeable about plants.

In his book *A Garden of Memories*, Ingram described how Johnston brought along "his chauffeur and his Italian valet/cook, which certainly added to his personal comfort but seemed to me to be a bit of an extravaganza. However, he was certainly active in the field." Always on the lookout for a garden worthy specimen, at one point as they drove along their route, Johnston spotted "a plant of superlative beauty. A plant we simply must collect at all costs." Ingram carries on to describe how Johnston stopped the car and rushed back, climbed the steep slope toward the "crimson coloured bloom of some unknown Liliaceous species," only to discover it was a piece of red paper blown there on the wind. Perhaps Ingram's description should have read "enthusiastic" rather than "active."

A year later, Johnston was scrambling around Mount Kilimanjaro, where he discovered a fine hypericum (today *Hypericum* 'Hidcote' is a favorite yellow-flowered shrub in mixed borders). That trip inspired Johnston's only known attempt at garden writing, in which he described the beauty he found in ugliness (of the *Senecio johnstonii*) and the miniature flower gardens he discovered tucked away in the mountain's gullies. Today we would call them microclimates, but the result is the same—more plants.

His least successful expedition was made in 1930 to Yunnan, China, with George Forrest, not the easiest man to get along with at the best of times. But Johnston, with his gentlemanly ways, did nothing to help himself, it would seem, for Forrest complained in a letter to one of the expedition's backers, "He was too busy gadding around . . . riding in the morning, tea and tennis in the afternoons and bridge at the club in the evening." Nonetheless, Johnston collected *Jasminum polyanthum,* which many gardeners cherish for its fine perfume, and *Mahonia lomarifolia* and *M. siamensis,* which became extremely popular among gardeners for their fine foliage, elegant flowers, and fine scents.

Johnston was taken ill and left the Forrest expedition in early 1931; later that same year he sought to join an expedition to Formosa but decided to subscribe only, put off perhaps by the expedition leader, Kan Yashiroda, who explained (in fractured English) that the natives were not friendly: "They proud very much that their house are decorated by many craniums of the foreign who were killed by them."

The material Johnston brought home or received from subscriptions was given to his gardener, Frank Adams, to propagate, and in 1929 a selection was sent to the Royal Botanic Gardens, Edinburgh, with accompanying notes describing each plant, where it was found, and at what altitude. These included a species of giant lobelia from the "Kilimanjaro Forest. 4000. In open spaces, full sun, semitropical. Tall branching tree lobelia, 10? or more high. . . . A curious but ornamental plant.?" Another lobelia was described as being "?1 yard high . . . Kilimanjaro 12000? 13000? . . . growing in peaty, acid soil in full exposure to sun and wind amongst dwarf heather. Will certainly stand some frost. . . . Fine large flowered Hypericum from Kilimanjaro 12000? . . . One of the best things I found."

In common with many amateur plant-hunters at that time, Johnston was concerned with expanding the range of plant material that could be grown in the gardens of the northern hemisphere; thus the mountain ranges of Africa, China, India, and Persia were their prime hunting grounds, since the conditions of these temperate regions most closely simulated those in European gardens.

Norah Warre, a close friend whose house, Villa Roquebrune, and sumptuous garden were near Serre de la Madone, recalled how Lawrence was always generous with the plants he collected, distributing them

Garden ornaments at Serre de la Madone recall Johnston's decorative collection at Hidcote. Jacques Lanteri

among friends—particularly if he thought they would fare better in their gardens than in his own, because of aspect, soil, or some such difference. Norah Warre's garden had an entirely different aspect and terrain, so she often received treasures from him with the explanation, as she recalled, "My plants may not live, so if yours do I can come over to admire them." He gave Mrs. Warre specimens he brought back from expeditions or raised from subscribers' seed allocations, including one of Kingdon-Ward's finest contributions, *Meconopsis betonicifolia*), the Tibetan blue poppy. Today that flower grows thickly in the beds around the Bathing Pool. There is a story that Norah Lindsay had one of the first garden specimens at Sutton Courtenay, and so envious was Lady Oxford (Margot Asquith, a Lindsay neighbor and another of the Souls) that she lifted it to her own garden. Norah Warre claimed that Johnston also plant-hunted in Mexico, a trip he may have undertaken before the one to China, or perhaps he simply subscribed to it, buying shares to finance the trip and receiving a portion of the seed gathered. The Mexican collection was housed in a special area of the garden at Serre de la Madone, while plants from the other expeditions were scattered throughout the garden.

Johnston's passion for plant-collecting caused him to become increasingly involved with his French garden, since in its sympathetic climate he was able to grow a wider range of choice plants than could be grown in the comparatively harsh Cotswolds. At Hidcote, Lawrence had the Summer House (now called the Plant House); at Serre de la Madone a similar house was called the Winter House. Like Hidcote, his French garden had a southwest-facing aspect, and once again he exercised his talent as a designer, creating a series of terraces and hedged enclosures, pools, and vistas that were as near to Hidcote as he could make them.

The terraces at Serre de la Madone step down the slope below the cream-colored villa and are broken with flights of stone stairs, which are

Serre de la Madone, Johnston's property in the south of France, 2007. Jacques Lanteri

The main axis at Serre de la Madone descends the hillside in a series of terraces. 2007.
Jacques Lanteri

themselves broken by fountains, a characteristic of many Mediterranean gardens that have taken their design from the classic gardens of Italy. Intermittent landings break the fall of the terraces and on one, midway down the site, is a single lily pool, bisected by the continuation of the main axis that continues down the slope, finishing at a rondel of box in the middle of one of the lower terraces. Previously, each terrace had its own character taken from the plants used there: succulents, clematis arbor, and a huge aviary that was once an integral part of the estate—another echo of Hidcote. Peacocks, ibis, crested cranes, macaws, and other exotica added to Johnston's private Eden. Statuary and urns, busts and treillage abounded. By the sound of this description, Norah's assessment of Serre de la Madone's unfocused clutter was not far off the mark.

Time was not kind to Serre de la Madone; the property went through a succession of owners after Johnston's death. The owner at the time of writing the first edition of this book was determined to sell it for development into condominiums and so was adamant in her refusal to allow "botanists" (and this author) into the garden. But on December

Bathing pool terrace at Serre de la Madone, 2007. Jacques Lanteri

12, 1990, Serre de la Madone was classified as a Monument Historique by the French government, and a rescue operation was initiated with cooperation from the European Community, and the Ministry of Culture and Environment of the General Council of the Alpes-Maritimes. Peter Dennis, a former National Trust gardener at Hidcote, was involved early on with the move to rescue Serre de la Madone, and he described the garden a few years after the government intervention: "You can only see the bones of the garden, as it has taken the past few years to reclaim the structure from what had literally become a jungle. There is still a lot of clearing to do, but the next phase is to begin gathering together the huge variety of plants that once grew in the garden."

An article in *Country Life* (July 10, 1986) by the horticultural jour-

One of several cross-axial views and remnants of Johnston's extensive plant collections gathered from subtropical zones in South Africa, China, and on his own doorstep in Provence, 2007. Jacques Lanteri

nalist Fred Whitsey, described the remnants of the original planting, which in the kind Mediterranean climate seems to have in many cases flourished to such a degree that the garden was in danger of disappearing beneath a mantle of naturalized exotica. In his day, Johnston had a team of gardeners under the leadership of Henry Lloyd, who replaced Frensham. Will Ingwersen, who was one of England's foremost authorities on alpine plants, was employed at Serre de la Madone in the early years of that garden. His father was a friend of Johnston who, on hearing that the young Ingwersen was looking for work experience abroad, suggested he help in the making of Serre de la Madone. Ingwersen was there for a number of years, three of which were spent as head gardener. He recalls that Johnston cut short his expedition with Forrest, because

The yellow rose 'Lawrence Johnston' climbs the villa walls; with single yellow blooms the size of saucers, it has pronounced red stamens and a light, fruity perfume and will ramble up a support in no time. 2007. Jacques Lanteri

the two men did not get along at all well, and that a frequent visitor was Edith Wharton, the American novelist whose book *Italian Villas and Their Gardens,* published in 1904, was one of the first books in over a hundred years to be devoted entirely to that subject. As a result, it soon became, in her words, "a working manual for architectural students and landscape gardeners."

Edith Wharton, as mentioned in Chapter One, was from the same old New York society as Johnston, and their shared love of gardening probably consolidated the friendship. Wharton became an expatriate on her divorce from her husband, Teddy Wharton. Leaving her home, The Mount, in Lenox, Massachusetts, in 1912, she settled in Paris, first in an apartment at 53 Rue Varenne, then in 1920 moved into the elegant small manor house Pavillon Colombe at Saint-Brice. Immediately, she set about creating a comfortable, modern home surrounded by formal gardens well suited to the late-eighteenth-century architecture of the Pavillon. Her old friend Bernard Berenson's villa, I Tatti, at Settignano in the hills south-west of Florence, was a model of modernity allied to classic style; it may well have inspired Wharton's own effort—indeed, she did at one point consult Berenson's architect, Cecil Pinsent. She also called upon her friend Lawrence Johnston, who helped her to plant a parterre with solid blocks of blue hyacinth surrounded by little clipped box hedges.

In 1920, Wharton also began leasing a property in the south of France, where she wintered and fell in love with the climate and the plants—both so very different and exotic compared to the tame and chilly northern zones she knew. The place was called Château Sainte-Claire at Hyères. Located on a hillside overlooking the town, the villa was built from the ruins of a medieval convent. Edith began to garden there, too, but in a style very different from the formal, historically correct manner of her Parisian garden.

Edith Wharton on the steps of her garden at Château Sainte-Claire in the hills above Hyères; she and Johnston shared a common heritage as well as a love of gardening and were frequent visitors at each other's homes. From Alice Martineau's *Gardening in Sunny Lands*, 1924.

Maryland, Cap Ferrat. Gardens in the south of France were inclined to be more natural; gardens existed, to paraphrase Edith Wharton, for the plants they held rather than the other way around. It was a more picturesque effect and a reflection of the expatriate community's romance with the south. From *Gardening in Sunny Lands*, 1924.

Lawrence Johnston was a frequent visitor to Wharton's French properties, staying for lengthy periods, sometimes up to three weeks, even when he had his own French villa and garden. Likewise, Wharton would motor over to Menton and Serre de la Madone for a visit. Often, Norah Lindsay would be in residence, or would come with "Johnny" to Sainte-Claire. Together they would exchange plants, garden plans, and visits with other expatriate gardeners who populated the Riviera. One of these, Basil Leng, became the "guru" to the garden set of the south of France, and many plants cultivated at his garden, at Socoa, Saint-Jean-de-Luz, found their way into gardens all along the southern coast of France. Leng's garden was exceptional for its seaside location, beginning as a stretch of clay cliff between the headland and the sea. Leng added much sand to improve the soil and so made it an ideal nursery for tender and exotic bulbs, while terracing and the construction of protective walls opened possibilities for tender perennials.

Another of Johnston's friends in France, who lived for a time near Edith Wharton's home at Hyères, was Charles, Vicomte de Noailles, who had made a garden around the house he built just after the First World War. Several years later, he began work on a new garden around a seventeenth-century villa at Grasse in the Alpes-Maritimes.

Built, like Serre de la Madone, on the terraces of olive grove and vineyard, the vicomte used water to link the component "rooms" of his plan: "Here," he said, "everything centers on water from the source." There is more than an echo of Hidcote at Villa Noailles. The lawn terrace with twin gazebos and mixed borders seems to be a deliberate *homage* to Johnston's English garden, which is also recalled by the peony terrace: the Pillar Garden at Hidcote was thickly planted with the many varieties of peonies that Johnston so keenly collected.

Johnston often played squash and tennis with the vicomte at Villa Noailles and the two men planned a plant-hunting expedition to Burma. But with war looming in 1938 this scheme was canceled, as were Johnston's winter sojourns at Serre de la Madone. He was there, however, when the Germans invaded northern France; then the Italians entered the war, and he was caught on that front too, but was evacuated in 1940. Mark Fenwick described Johnston's return in a letter to E. A. Bowles: "Johnnie came back in the Collier, the story of which Somerset Maugham gave on a broadcast two or three weeks ago. He looked quite well and apparently had thrived on coal dust which was about all he had to eat. He had to leave the menagerie behind and seemed to mind the loss of his dogs far more than the Villa or gardens."

In fact, Charles de Noailles knew Lawrence Johnston many years before the former settled at Grasse. At Varengeville near Dieppe in Normandy, Edwin Lutyens designed alterations for a nineteenth-century villa, commissioned by a young man named Guillaume Mallet. Mallet's interests were in the Arts and Crafts mold: he was a talented amateur artist and botanist and had made several journeys through England and Italy accompanied by his mother.

Mallet's house is called Le Bois des Moutiers, and the gardens were made strictly according to the principles of Lutyens's collaborator,

(right and opposite) Views of the terraced gardens at Villa Noailles, which are located near Johnston's own garden, Serre de la Madone, in the Val de Gorbio above Menton, France, 1998. Ethne Clarke

Gertrude Jekyll (whose design for a huge perennial border was never implemented). Mallet, like Johnston, was a perfectionist when it came to realizing the plans for his garden, and he is said to have used scraps of eighteenth-century textiles to decide the color scheme of the planting.

Johnston obviously knew of the garden and that it would be an ideal situation for the cultivation of rhododendrons, and so sent a gift of seed of several sorts to Mallet. Charles de Noailles served as the courier; he was eighteen at the time.

Basil Leng was a frequent contributor to *Country Life* and other gardening publications, but as publicity had no attractions for Johnston, Serre de la Madone was not one of his subjects, and Johnston kept his public profile in the south of France as low as he did in England. May-

bud Campbell, who was one of the most distinguished gardeners in Menton, recalled that Johnston was once pointed out to her at the tennis club, but until then she had had no idea that he owned a garden.

Johnston only opened his garden at Hidcote for charity, but never entered any of the Royal Horticultural Society shows, at least not while he was in residence at Hidcote. In 1949, after the National Trust had assumed the care of the gardens and Johnston was based at Serre de la Madone, he agreed to Albert Hawkins (then the nominal head gardener) entering a collection of pelargoniums and offered to pay his expenses. But the need to touch all the bases with the National Trust's administration made Hawkins late with his application. Nevertheless, Hawkins scrapped in and won a bronze medal, even though the exhibit was generally considered (by the Trust) to be a "very poor one." In 1956, Sir Anthony and Lady Eden allowed their names to be given to two hybrid pelargoniums raised at Hidcote.

But within the exclusive circles of the horticultural establishment, Johnston gained early recognition. Apart from his election in 1922 to the Garden Society, in 1947, Johnston was awarded a Gold Veitch Memorial Medal, given by the Royal Horticultural Society in recognition of outstanding contributions to horticulture. In Johnston's case, the numerous introductions of new plants for which he was responsible was just one of his outstanding contributions.

In the south of France, Johnston's influence on garden design was not as widespread as it was in England, although one last garden, Le Clos du Peyronnet, has Hidcotean features, the most obvious being, in the words of its present owner, William Waterfield, "a small garden within a garden hedged with cypress and almost completely filled by a pool." The villa and garden were created over a period of more than sixty years, beginning in 1915, although the garden was relandscaped after the Second World War by Humphrey Waterfield.

If Hidcote successfully resolved the argument between the formal and natural schools of garden design, it also laid the foundations of what was to become the preoccupation of most garden owners: the display of plant collections. The actual design of the garden for the provision of a pretty pictorial display had long been the overriding concern for most people involved with gardening, but from the end of the First World War, a new criteria was established. With the ever-expanding selection of plant material arriving from all over the world, garden enthusiasts became plant enthusiasts and the Hidcote style was seen to be the perfect setting for the appreciation and, most important, the successful cultivation of plant collections. By its arrangement of "rooms," it permitted an enormously varied selection of plants to be grown, but without sacrificing the repose that is more easily achieved in a garden where the variety of planting is restrained by the need to avoid a cluttered, spotty feeling.

Johnston furnished his garden rooms so that only specific parts of the garden were of interest at specific times of the year. For example, in the spring, the lilacs in the Old Orchard and the peonies in the Pillar Garden were the main attractions. In midsummer, the Red Border would blaze away; in autumn Westonbirt beckoned. Johnston also saw that every season has its own natural color theme, as can be seen in early spring in the Stream Garden, where blue and yellow predominate.

By arranging the garden in this fashion, Johnston placed a natural restraint on the amount of labor and expense required to maintain the garden (an important consideration for Johnston, who once remarked to Norah Warre, "I haven't got a bean"); it is easier to maintain parts of the whole some of the time than the whole thing all of the time. At most, in later years, there were only five full-time gardeners, though this could swell to ten when conditions demanded it. Additionally, and perhaps unconsciously, he reinforced the architectural qualities of the garden by having positive areas (where plants were flowering) and negative (where they were not). These were just some of the ideas that were borrowed by Johnston's friends in the designing of their own gardens.

There are two gardens in the north of England in which the owners' friendship with Lawrence Johnston is recognized as having had a marked influence. Both gardens were planned as a sequence of garden rooms, which are glimpsed through openings in the hedge-made walls, and with each area bearing its own color and planting character.

At Newby Hall, near Ripon in North Yorkshire, the gardens surround a superb Adam house; it has been said that Adam created a feeling of movement in his architectural design by the diversity of rooms, each of which had its particular purpose and so was quite unlike its neighbors. So in this curious way, the garden exterior can be thought to reflect the domestic interior.

In its earlier incarnation, the garden was pure Victoriana, with, in 1906, a formal terrace with a scroll parterre of box, bedding, and gravel paths laid before the library windows. From this balustraded terrace, replete with urns and statuary, a sweep of lawn rolled down to the river Ure. The grass was cut into a collection of shaped beds, "arched and enframed with ivy."

All this was swept away by Captain Edward Compton, who was influenced by his friend Johnston to replace the parterre terrace with simple lawns and a formal pool, to create a long grass walk to replace the ivy-framed beds, and to edge the walk with broad herbaceous borders, planted in bold blocks of color; dark yew hedges behind the beds enhance the vibrant display. Norah Lindsay designed these borders. This is the main access to the other parts of the garden and, just as at Hidcote, with the long avenue from Cedar Lawn to the Stilt Garden, the other garden rooms open off this main corridor and a group of fine beech trees provides the focus for the garden plan.

The long borders run from the south front of the house down to the riverfront. On either side of the main avenue, rooms open off and the crossing vistas terminate in statuary or a well-grown tree. One of the areas on the western side of the main avenue is today designated the Autumn Garden, and a golden carpet of fallen beech leaves shines in its background. The remainder is devoted to shrubs and trees for autumn color and scent. Along the eastern side, a rose garden is partnered by an enclosure dominated by beech trees, below which a curved pergola leads into a magnificent rockery. Here a series of rock pools play between screens of bamboo and evergreen foliage. Below the east front of the house is a small secret garden.

Further north, near Richmond, North Yorkshire, the Honorable Robert James created the gardens around St. Nicholas. The house commands a wonderful view from the terrace at the entrance. The garden rooms, however, are arranged to the side and behind the house. Bobbie James and Johnston were close friends and frequent guests at each other's houses. Like Lawrence, he was a talented artist, as was his brother, Lord Northbourne, whose expertise as a watercolorist contributed to the success of his garden, Northbourne Court, Kent.

At St. Nicholas, Mr. James and his wife, Lady Serena, gathered about them many garden-loving friends, including E. A. Bowles, Norah Lindsay, and Lawrence. Guests would arrive, Lady Serena recalled, bearing boxes of plants, bags of seed, and countless cuttings.

James was a plantsman first and foremost, and although an artist in arranging the color plan of the double borders, he incorporated many specimen plants alongside the more everyday herbaceous flowers. As at Hidcote, the garden is divided by yew hedges and retaining walls, which also mark the variation in level between one part of the garden and another. The property lies along a ridge that drops down to a river, and in the farthest corner Mr. James, with the help of Ellen Willmott, made a rock garden that is entered through a collection of the rhododendrons and the other calcifuge plants that he loved; like Johnston, Mr. James had to create pockets of acid soil to accommodate these plants. One area of the garden, known as the Cottage Garden, was Lady Serena's domain and contained a comprehensive collection of old-fashioned shrub roses and numerous species of lilies arranged in rectangular beds divided by paths of York paving.

Whereas Johnston's Red Borders peaked in August, the plants in James's borders followed spring and summer, beginning with the cool blues of early summer, the tints warming as the season progressed. Beyond the borders lay the Old Orchard, bisected by a grass walk between spring borders planted with masses of iris and tulips, planned to flower along with the fruit-tree blossoms. Summer's end was received in the small enclosure beyond the orchard where the four sides of a square lawn were bordered by grey foliage plants like artemisia and *Stachys lanata* that also provided a foil for red-flowered penstemon, phlox, and *Lobelia cardinalis*.

Another garden that smacks soundly of Hidcote is the Courts at Holt, near Trowbridge in Wiltshire. Again, a series of garden rooms is linked by a long walk, along which are ranged a number of sentinel yews. As one walks along, the other garden areas are spied between the yews' mass as sudden bursts of color. It was made by Lady Cecile Goff beginning in 1920; she intended the garden to be full of surprises and, just as at Hidcote, one must always pass through dark hedges and follow the path's turn to discover one garden after another. One of the most stunning is the Long Walk, where a grass runner stretches the length between a pair of mixed borders of herbaceous plants and shrubs. One end of the walk is graced with a small temple, its front regarding the front of the

main house. Not surprisingly, this is the main axis of the garden, recalling Hidcote's long walk and twin gazebos.

Tintinhull is a more recent creation, established in 1933 by Mrs.
Phyllis Reiss. She and her husband, Captain F. E. Reiss, had made a garden at Dowdeswell near Cheltenham in which they experimented with
the garden style of their friend and mentor, Lawrence Johnston. Like
Johnston, Mrs. Reiss was a devotee of the Italian Renaissance garden; she
had traveled in Italy and no doubt studied the design of these gardens
firsthand.

When she came to Tintinhull in 1933, she found that the basic structure of the garden was already there, and within that framework she was
able to create what Tintinhull's former custodian, Penelope Hobhouse,
called "a Hidcote in miniature; two acres instead of ten."

From the house front, a main walk leads through a series of three
individual garden areas. This central axis is studded with pudding-shaped
yews that mirror each other the length of the path. The walk terminates
in a small pool within a hedged enclosure, and as one strolls along,
glimpses of the other areas can be seen through small openings in wall
and hedge.

Mrs. Reiss, while fully cognizant of Miss Jekyll's color theory for the
successful planting of herbaceous borders, made much better use of the
flowers by planting them in bold masses of contrasting pure color, à la
Norah Lindsay, and unified the borders by repeat plantings of grey
foliage plants in the front and tall grasses at the back. At Hidcote, the
clumps of daylily foliage in the foreground of the Red Border serve the
same purpose, and during Johnston's day, the back of the border was
planted with clumps of pampas grass.

Mrs. Reiss understood the importance of restraint, and while the garden at Tintinhull is as lush and full as one could hope, the repetition of
color schemes (purple and yellow especially) and the repeated use of certain shrubs, like cultivars of the smoke bush, *Cotinus coggygria,* give the
garden a firm architectural base.

One last garden must be mentioned, and that is Kiftsgate Court. The
entrance to its drive faces the drive to Hidcote, and its creator, Heather
Muir, and her family were close friends of Major Johnston.

Kiftsgate occupies a startling position on a north-facing scarp, peer-
ing out over the Vale of Evesham. It must have taken a great deal of

courage and determination to establish a garden in such an exposed position. Only by planting a number of hedge-enclosed rooms could Mrs.
Muir hope to succeed. And this she did, borrowing the idea of a strong
architectural layout from her neighbor's property but putting her own
stamp on the scheme, for at Kiftsgate the garden seems to exist solely for
the plants it contains, rather than as it is at Hidcote, where the planting
is chiefly intended to serve the garden design. From the full-blown lux-
uriance of Kiftsgate, it appeared that Mrs. Muir believed, as did William
Robinson, that the best aspects of a plant could be realized only by allowing it to follow its natural inclinations in a natural setting.

Behind the house are the formal areas of the White Garden and the
area known as the Four Squares, where the space is quartered by crossing paths. Stretching away from the White Garden to the northeast is the
double rose border, where an enormous variety of old shrub roses are
grown, some of them massive specimens of these excellent plants. Behind
one side of the rose border is the Yellow Border, where golden flowers
are set off by rich blues and purple-leaved shrubs. From these formal
areas, along grand walks or through little cuts, one reaches the wilder
parts of the garden that tumble down the slope and which are packed
with an enormous range of specimen shrubs and trees, all grown to their
full stature and enhancing the naturalness of the setting. Since I wrote
this description for the first edition, Kiftsgate has undergone renovation
and new areas have been added by the family. That is another point of
difference between it and Hidcote; while Kiftsgate continues to develop
guided by descendants of the people who created it, the National Trust's
chief purpose of the Hidcote renovation was to bring it back to a sem-
blance of its appearance in the 1930s, the period the Trust has identified
as being the garden's prime. The Trust, as Hidcote's custodians, does
look to the future, of course, but of necessity is always mindful of the
backward glance.

Four

THE LATER YEARS

Throughout the 1930s, life at Hidcote continued at an even pace; even the ravages of the Depression made little impression on the well-being of the little hamlet. The manor, farm, and garden provided employment for most of the families, and also food, since Lawrence allowed his staff to take all the vegetables, fruit, eggs, and milk they wanted from the produce surplus to his own needs. During the winter months, when Johnston was in France, this amounted to much of what was grown. Later, during the Second World War, the huge kitchen garden at Hidcote supplied four large hospitals with fresh produce.

The Second World War was hard on Hidcote, however. Johnston was evacuated from his French home in 1940. The journey was arduous and fraught with danger, yet evacuated to England on a coal ship, he was among one of the last group of expatriate evacuees. He arrived exhausted, dirty, and disoriented. Johnston was then sixty-nine years old; his health was failing and his mental condition was faltering, and by 1942 he was beginning to suffer, as his mother had, from the onset of dementia. In Johnston's case, he suffered long bouts of total amnesia and periods of profound confusion.

In common with many large properties that had been subjected to the government policy of billeting Allied forces at country houses, Hidcote housed a troop of American soldiers. Many of the local men from

The lane running through Hidcote village looking toward the manor house, c. 1907; its chimneys are visible just behind the trees.

Mickleton and Hidcote were away at war, and thus the armed forces in their various ways took its toll on the condition of the garden.

There is a story that before Johnston was evacuated from France he had wired back to Albert Hawkins to grub up the 'Frau Karl Drushki' roses that filled the beds in the little garden room next to the Bathing Pool and to replace them with fuchsias. The Germans were at war with his adopted homeland, and Lawrence would not abide any reference to that country in his precious garden. He cannot have been aware, in that case, of the origins of the fuchsia's name: after Leonhart Fuchs, the sixteenth-century German botanist.

At this time, the Major, having left his shuttered property and dispersed his menagerie at Serre de la Madone, gathered about him at Hidcote a pack of seven dachshunds. These small, nervy dogs followed him everywhere, chasing about, nipping at his heels and those of visitors to Hidcote. He was continually shouting at them, but they came in handy for chasing rabbits. One of Lawrence's godsons (he had at least two) recalls that when he and his young wife stayed as guests at Hidcote, they in their wing, Lawrence in his, they would all meet on the lawn in the early morning to chase rabbits with the dachshunds. Johnston had always had dogs, it would seem, and the first animals at Hidcote were English spaniels with the simple names Timmy and Ricky. In Westonbirt, he had the flamingos and the ostrich in the aviary; the incongruity of these exotic birds striding through maples in an English woodland garden gives pause for thought. It is also an indication of Lawrence's whole-hearted pursuit of his enthusiasms. It would seem that Lawrence was ful-filling his desired destiny by becoming a dotty old English bachelor of military bearing, living out his years in a crumbly stone manor attended by a devoted gaggle of lifelong retainers and absorbed totally in the con-tinued cultivation of the manor house garden, his sole creation.

In 1939, Johnston's right-hand man in the garden, Frank Adams, died. Johnston had always said that it would be impossible for him to replace Adams, and indeed, he never did hire another head gardener. Instead he resumed the mantle, but looked on Albert Hawkins, who had been in charge of the kitchen garden, as his overseer, responsible for coordinating with the other gardeners: Ted Pearce, Walter Bennett, and Sid Nicholls.

However, without the professionalism instilled by Frank Adams, and because of the other gardeners' reluctance to be organized by the kitchen gardener, Hidcote began to look rather tired and out of focus. Although Lawrence had a cordial relationship with his staff, and they were all devoted to him, it was on occasions a case of the tail wagging the dog.

It's uncertain when it occurred to Lawrence that he would have to make some provision for Hidcote if it was to survive. He had no imme-diate kin to whom the estate would pass; in the terms of Gertrude's will, Hidcote was his exclusively, and in any case, his main concern would have been for the preservation of the garden.

On February 5, 1943, Lawrence attended a luncheon party given by Sybil, Lady Colefax. She, however, was ill and her friend, Norah Lindsay, was deputizing as hostess. Another guest was James Lees-Milne, who at that time was serving as, in his words, "an unqualified historic buildings secretary" for the National Trust.

The National Trust was established in 1895 as conservators of Britain's finest landscape and architectural heritage. In the early 1940s, almost fifty years after its founding, the Trust supported approximately 75,000 acres and six country houses and had a membership of 6,000. It fulfilled its charter largely through the endeavors of a small devoted team committed to the Trust and whose work was in those "distant war days a combination of hard labor and sheer fun. Distinction between one and the other was seldom absolute." Mr. Lees-Milne's sentiment, here quoted, is clarified by the diaries he made during those years and in which he describes Johnston enquiring of him, at Sybil Colefax's luncheon, whether the National Trust would take over the garden after the war, as he was planning to return then to France to live permanently.

Johnston was friendly with Lees-Milne's father, and as a child, James had visited Hidcote on several occasions. Johnston was over a quarter of a century older than Lees-Milne, who found him a "dull little man . . . Mother-ridden. Mrs. Winthrop, swathed in grey satin from neck to ankle, would never let him out of her sight." James Pope-Hennessy, also a guest at that luncheon, called Johnston a "Howard Sturgis American." (Sturgis's parents were wealthy expatriate Americans and he was a dedicated Anglophile. At his home, Queen's Acre, near Windsor, Sturgis entertained a catholic collection of friends, including Edith Wharton and Lawrence Johnston. This is a rather loaded remark as Sturgis wrote a poorly received, somewhat embarrassing novel, *Belchamber*, of which his friend Henry James asked "why did he do it?" Pope-Hennessy seems to be suggesting that Johnston was not quite the caliber of a "Henry James American.")

Four months after the luncheon party, on July 6, Lawrence received James Lees-Milne and his father for tea and took them around the garden, without referring to the question of the Trust's possible interest. Lees-Milne found the garden wonderfully full of delightful interludes and exotic plants and expressed surprise that such a varied garden could be contained within so few acres. But as he listened to his father and Johnston converse, what impressed him the most was "their profound knowledge of a subject which is closed to me." Lees-Milne likened it to overhearing a conversation in a foreign language unknown to him. This is a common memory of the people who knew Johnston: that when encountered socially, he was a man of limited conversation, unless it turned to gardening, when he became immediately at ease and, at times, even animated.

The National Trust was still taking shape at that time and had no gardens under its care that were not attached to a property. And for them to consider taking on an unendowed property, one that would come, in effect, with a begging-bowl, looking for support, was distinctly unlikely. Initially, the Trust relied solely on benefaction and members' subscriptions, plus whatever the properties could earn through public admission fees. The war years, and those postwar, were particularly difficult. The paying public had more pressing concerns.

Johnston had no private capital with which to endow Hidcote; he lived off the interest of a share of Gertrude's estate, and that share would, on his death, revert to the estate. Such was his resentment over the treatment he received by the terms of his mother's will that he was unwilling to leave Hidcote to any of his cousins.

And he still had his French property to tend, and finance. Serre de la Madone was occupied by the Italians during the war, but after their surrender in 1943, Johnston was eventually able to return; there he found that most of the furnishings had been looted and the gardens extensively damaged.

Johnston's advancing illness and old age was being reflected in the condition of the gardens he had made. It is a fact that the best gardens are those tended by one caring and devoted person, preferably the person whose inspiration it was to create the garden in the first place. But when that guiding light begins to dim, and it is left largely to the staff to do as they think best, often in straitened circumstances, the integrity of the garden begins to weaken.

Nothing more was said about the National Trust for several years as Johnston struggled along as best he could. The European war ended on May 7, 1945, and just over one year later, James Lees-Milne was back at Hidcote, assessing the property and the hamlet. He found Lawrence "old and ill" and could not see how the National Trust could ever maintain Hidcote with only five gardeners and, most pertinently, without an endowment.

Later that year, he was back at Hidcote in the company of Harold Nicolson and Vita Sackville-West. The couple had spent a week touring the West Country, visiting stately homes—often unannounced—and eating rather poorly at their various lodgings.

To their dismay, when they arrived at Hidcote at 2:30 P.M., they found the lunch table laid for four and Johnston peeved that the "succulent meal" he had made for his guests was wasted. Nevertheless, he must have forgiven them easily enough, charmed no doubt by Vita's ability to speak the garden-lover's language. They made a quick round of the garden, Vita was given a mass of cuttings, and they took their leave in order to be at Charlecote Park near Stratford-on-Avon by 4 P.M.

In April 1947, Sybil Colefax wrote with some urgency to James Lees-Milne, "Lawrie Johnston wants to give Hidcote to the National Trust now—so do get him tied up. You see he is not 'gaga,' but has no memory." Johnston had been making plans to leave Hidcote to Bill Barrington, 10th Viscount Barrington, who lived at Nether Lypiatt Manor in a comfortable ménage with Violet and Gordon Woodhouse. He was an artist and erstwhile garden designer and had made beautiful gardens at Nether Lypiatt very much in the Hidcote mold. But Barrington did not want Hidcote, and when Johnston discovered this, he was in a quandary. But at Sybil Colefax's urging, he once again considered the National Trust.

Although he was ill when Lady Colefax saw him, he was, she thought, "bright as a button," and his mind was, for the time being, focused on the Trust taking Hidcote. But given the vagaries of his mental condition, she urged speed and suggested ways of overcoming the financial difficulties, such as selling the house, the farm, the kitchen garden. Both she and Lees-Milne realized that it would be an unmitigated disaster if the garden was left to someone who did not want it and who would then be likely to sell it immediately.

Britain was fortunate in having the services of James Lees-Milne and his equally dedicated colleagues. Their conviction of the necessity—the obligation we have—to maintain, and in many cases salvage, our architectural heritage, and their ability to see beyond the forest of difficulties with which such causes are always fraught, set Britain above most other countries in richness and variety of landscape, built and natural. Lees-Milne may not have been able to conjure a National Trust future for an unendowed Hidcote, but he felt compelled to try. The Trust had never taken on a garden; previously, gardens came as part of an estate, with the house as the central feature. Hidcote was different. The house was pretty enough, but unremarkable. However, the garden made the exception and, even then, was recognized as seminal to the development of English landscape design. As Lees-Milne wrote in his report to the National Trust, "As a specimen of the twentieth-century garden, this one at Hidcote is fasci-

Hidcote Manor, c. 1972. Seymour Preston

nating and probably unsurpassed." But he had to underline the fact that "unfortunately, gardens are ephemeral things, unless money is fairly lavishly spent." And there was not a great deal of money available to lavish.

The Historic Buildings Committee of the National Trust accepted Lees-Milne's assessment and strongly recommended that the Trust take on Hidcote with the proviso that adequate endowment would be forthcoming and that the gardens would be property maintained under the supervision of a curator or custodian holding suitable horticultural qualifications.

While the committee was considering its recommendation, Johnston was considering his future: "I don't want to make it over to them now as I want to be master in my own place as long as I live here. It is an easy place to let as it is not too big, but of course the garden is expencive [*sic*] to keep up." He must have realized that the Trust was contemplating the rent that could be obtained from the house and figured that they would only accept his garden if he gave them the house. He had himself considered renting Hidcote while living, as Norah Lindsay postulated, in a tent in the garden.

The White Garden is one of the earliest parts of the garden, c. 1986. Ethne Clarke

These early documents reveal what was going to be the leitmotif of the entire Hidcote–National Trust transfer. The Trust was dealing with an elderly, confused, ailing man who was distracted by the uncertain future of his masterpiece, dependent upon an institution for its salvation, yet unwilling to accept the terms that would for them make the transaction feasible. Repeatedly, the Trust was faced with trying to satisfy their trustees and satisfy Johnston.

Not unreasonably, one of the first avenues they tried when seeking financial assistance was the Royal Horticultural Society. Harold Nicolson approached them but was met with a flat refusal. As Lord Aberconway explained, the RHS "could not provide funds for a garden rather remote from most of our fellows," nor could it offer any professional horticultural expertise to "keep the garden as it should be."

Nicolson wrote: "If we are to save Hidcote we shall have to try again. PS, I think the next action is to try Kew." However, that plea, even though it fell on sympathetic ears, was unsuccessful.

In August, Herbert Smith, the chief agent of the National Trust, went to Hidcote to compile a financial profile and present alternative ways of financing the garden. He came up with several, including a fairy-tale ending of letting the house to a very rich tenant who also was a keen gardener, who would finance and tend the garden. Or the Trust could mount an elaborate publicity campaign in an effort to boost attendance revenues. However, this was thought to be impractical since the garden was remote, both geographically and intellectually, and was considered by the committee to be of a type that would only attract experts and connoisseurs!

Johnston left for his annual French sojourn in September, and the Hidcote case was put on the back burner. In January, he was back, although exceptionally frail and twice as worried about the garden's future. It must be remembered that although the committee had been urged to accept the gardens, it had not yet in fact done so. In desperation, as it was thought that Johnston would not live long, Lees-Milne pressed for the question to be settled and suggested that the Gardens Committee raise a fund to finance the transaction.

The Gardens Committee emerged directly out of the Hidcote dilemma, plus the fact that the Trust had been offered White Craggs, Westmorland. Its panel consisted of equal representation of both the National Trust and the Royal Horticultural Society, with the RHS to provide expert advice on the care and future of the gardens in the Trust's care. Lord Aberconway, as president of the RHS, was to take an active role in pushing through the acceptance of Hidcote garden sans house. His seat, Bodnant, in North Wales, was more renowned for the excellent quality of its garden than for its house, and this may have concentrated his mind on the importance of a precedent being set for the acceptance of properties outside the category of "architectural interest." Also elected to the first committee was Lord Rosse, whose garden at Nymans fell into this category; both these gardens are now safeguarded by the National Trust.

Once again, Hidcote was breaking new ground, setting the course for the National Trust's future preservation of gardens. But the very novelty of the situation led to misunderstandings as the Trust felt its way along; Johnston's periods of befuddlement did not make matters easier. At one point, Johnston expressed his pleasure at the way things were proceeding, remarking that after caring for the garden for so many years, he couldn't give it up entirely, yet old age made the prospect of residence on the Riviera quite pleasing.

There was another reason why the south of France was so comfortable. In June 1948, Lawrence wrote to Lord Aberconway: "If I am domiciled here [England] they take all my income in taxes, so I must be domiciled in France where I have a nice house and garden." Lawrence's income, derived only from the interest of Gertrude's estate, would have been ravaged by the postwar economy. So once again, France provided a less expensive home, where dollars and pounds went further and where the English tax system couldn't reach him. This was Lawrence's main reason for retiring to Serre de la Madone, and he may have seen the Trust's takeover of Hidcote as a way around the problem, if he could maneuver them into accepting the garden while allowing him to retain his rights to the house. To Aberconway, he again wrote: "Of course I should like it if I could come back here for short periods in the summer. There is so much I have planted that I should like to see grown. For that prevalidge [*sic*] I might be able to contribute to the expense. I should have to consult my lawyer about that. It all depends on whether I should make myself liable to English income tax. . . ."

The next day, he wrote again, but to the National Trust, enquiring rather hotly if he would be able to even *visit* Hidcote: "Shall I have any right of residence at Hidcote? I intend to live in France, but I might want to visit Hidcote. PS. This is an important point. If I have no right to the House I shall want to remove some furniture and family portraits."

Lees-Milne was given the job of smoothing Johnston's hackles and suggested that perhaps the easiest thing would be for him to leave Hidcote to the Trust by the terms of his will and in the meantime to retain Hidcote and meet all its expenses. Alternatively, Johnston could leave altogether and the Trust could install a supervisor.

Lawrence replied on June 19 that he was annoyed that he would be allowed nothing in return for the Trust's eventual entire possession of Hidcote and had decided he'd better keep it himself. He had visions of the RHS installing a head gardener and meeting the entire expenses for the privilege of its being open to the public and RHS members for a small fee to cover any extra expenses incurred. "As a matter of fact," he wrote, "I can do it myself by putting up a sign and letting my men collect the shillings. So perhaps we can call the whole thing off."

At this point, Lawrence seems to have lost sight of his original intention of providing for the future of Hidcote; his vision was obscured by

View of the Old Garden Border, c. 1973.
Seymour Preston

the specter of H.M. Inspector of Taxes and the prospect of letting go. Sybil Colefax, Lees-Milne, and Lord Aberconway all did their best to calm Johnston and to help him find a way out of his, and consequently their, dilemma: Johnston's desire to keep control of Hidcote would have clouded his position regarding liability to English taxes, as it may have been construed to constitute residence. Finally, Johnston's solicitors suggested a deed of gift presenting Hidcote to the Trust, but with a separate memorandum of wishes made that would give Johnston access to Hidcote for the rest of his life. If this were done, Lawrence might then be willing to contribute to the upkeep of Hidcote. However, he could not declare this intention formally, because it would lay him open to taxation.

This seemed to solve the problem, particularly from Lawrence's point of view. The wheels were set in motion, and the memorandum of wishes was drawn up, outlining the conditions of the transfer of Hidcote to the National Trust. Under its terms, Johnston retained the right to return to Hidcote at his pleasure, and the house would be maintained for his eventual visits. He was to be the uncontrolled supervisor of the gardens, which would be open not more than three times a week, particularly if he was in residence. And by giving away his English domicile, he was freed from the threat of double taxation, English and French.

While this satisfied Lawrence's wishes, the Trust was left without a house to rent and, during Johnston's lifetime at least, the income generated by renting. But it was a risk worth taking and one that should be reduced by spending the entire allowance of the garden fund on the garden (the fund had been earmarked for garden maintenance in any case).

For his part, Lawrence wrote to Lady Colefax expressing satisfaction, tinged however with sadness, at the outcome. He was leaving for France in September, where he intended to live, and would also be spending some time with Nancy Lindsay's brother Peter at his home in the French Alps.

One of Johnston's priorities when giving Hidcote into the care of the Trust was to see that the garden staff were allowed to carry on. In his view, they were all able men, completely attuned to his way of doing things and so more likely to maintain Hidcote as he wished it. As Johnston was his own head gardener, he realized that he would have to be replaced once he had retired to France. Albert Hawkins, because of his ability, was first in line for any possible promotion, but Lawrence explained the difficulties: that even though he thought Albert was a "brilliant gardener and plantsman with a good deal of taste," Lawrence reckoned that "he has not much head for planning ahead . . . he runs a big allotment and might give that priority . . . the other three [would not] stand Albert over them." But although he agreed that the hiring of a young head gardener would be the best solution, Johnston feared that such a man would be certain to alter the character of the garden.

Johnston signed the deed of gift at the end of August 1948 and left for France on September 14, taking all his dogs, his car, two servants, a quantity of plants from Kew, and a vanload of furniture. Before leaving, he reiterated his concern about installing a new head gardener: "I think it would be a pity to put in a strange head gardener. He would at once want to alter the whole scheme of the garden which in my mind would entirely spoil it." James Lees-Milne's memory of the occasion when Johnston finally signed over Hidcote paints a sad, somewhat melodramatic picture; Sybil Colefax was so worried about the garden's future that they "concocted a diabolical scheme," duping Johnston into signing the deed of gift by letting him think he was signing a different document. "I can recall the scene in the big downstairs room at Hidcote now while we the conspirators held our breath as he held the pen poised, and a shadow crossed his face and we feared for an awful second that he was going to jib. But he didn't."

Ultimately, the Trust accepted Johnston's request that Nancy Lindsay act as his deputy in the garden during his absence. This was a move that Nancy announced to Lees-Milne and Lord Esher as a *fait accompli* when they visited Hidcote in August just before the transfer was completed. They for their part were rather taken aback that she should assume that the Gardens Committee would accept this without question. However, if it came from Johnston, then it would have to be abided by (and there were suspicions that Nancy was putting words into Lawrence's mouth). It did solve to some degree the problem of appointing a head gardener.

Norah Lindsay died in 1948, another milestone in a year that for Lawrence was full of upheaval. Her daughter Nancy had spent a great deal of time at Hidcote and Serre de la Madone before and after the war and was closer to Johnston than she was to anyone else. He was quite obviously fond of her, and probably depended upon her to some extent and after Norah's death was particularly kind to her. In any event, he was confident enough of her abilities to make it a condition of the transfer, as explained by Mr. Garrett, Johnston's solicitor, that she "should in his absence and purely on his personal behalf act as general supervisor of the garden."

From the very outset, the Trust agreed that Nancy's involvement was to advise on the purely technical side of the garden only. Staff and other administrative arrangements were not to concern her in any way. There were, however, many shades of grey in this arrangement, and for the Trust, Nancy's nomination by Johnston was to cause more problems than it solved.

Like Lawrence, Nancy was a loner, and at her home, the Manor Cottage, Sutton Courtenay, which she inherited from Norah, she created her own world of plants, just as Johnston had done at Hidcote. Up to this time, Nancy had never had her own garden. But where his diffidence hid a likable social ability, Nancy's aloofness often presented itself as cranky eccentricity, and her quarrelsome nature made dealing with her exasper-

Nancy Lindsay in later years at around the time the National Trust was corresponding with her about Johnston's intentions regarding Hidcote.

ating. Yet those who knew Nancy best remember her as a loyal friend who positively enjoyed helping those she was fond of and generous with the little she had. Materially, Nancy was not well off, but her plants and her knowledge of how they should be grown were her wealth, and with that she was free.

In October, Nancy wrote to Lord Esher at the National Trust; he had been a close friend of her mother's, and Nancy was attempting to make Johnston's intentions for Hidcote "clear for anyone who is interested." It also seems she was trying to anticipate any awkwardness that might arise from her position as "a very old and devoted friend of Johnny's who knows Hidcote as well as he does himself," and explained that she saw her duty as ensuring that the status quo, "the lush and rather jungly effect that Johnny likes" would be maintained, at least in the short term, so that when he returned, he would find Hidcote unchanged, except for the improvements that he would direct through Nancy.

This was an appointment that she declared she was accepting out of love and for which her only recompense was to be "cuttings, seeds or 'throw-outs' from Hidcote," and she repeatedly emphasized the temporary nature of her position as "faithful watch-dog for Johnny." She also hoped that the Trust would find her a help and not a nuisance, especially as it was she who years ago had first persuaded Johnston to offer Hidcote to the Trust.

Lord Esher regarded the letter as "sinister" and Nancy's attitude as proprietary. It may well have been, since Nancy had treated the plants at Hidcote as a source of propagating material that she used to keep her own nursery stocked. But more than that, Nancy had known Johnston and Hidcote for many years, and there can be little doubt that she regarded the place as her own—a second home. In his dotage, and no doubt missing Norah, Johnston had grown quite fond of a woman named Ruth Peppercorn, who Nancy regarded as a rival. James Russell (the renowned English garden authority and plantsman), who knew Nancy through his sister, recalls that "the way Nancy said 'Ruthy Peppercorn' was like watching a cobra about to strike." It cannot have been easy for Nancy to watch Hidcote being handed over to what amounted to strangers, no matter how capable or concerned they may have been. And no one can deny the National Trust's ability and sincerity.

For their part, the Trust was faced with a whole host of problems and may have seen Nancy's contribution as interference in its efforts to deal with Hidcote efficiently. It was obliged to administer Hidcote as Johnston would have wished, but no doubt felt that it was in a better-informed position to make the decisions that would benefit all concerned. Furthermore, the Trust had numerous obligations to its other properties and would have wished to keep administration difficulties to a minimum. Nancy, on the other hand, beside her own garden, had only Hidcote to think about, and she would write "pamphlets" to the Trust officers, describing in repetitious detail the intricacies of running Hidcote.

Eventually, it was decided that a management committee should be established that would include Nancy. This idea was presented to Johnston in November 1948 in a letter from Lord Aberconway. He also said that it had been decided that the gardens would be open on Tuesday, Wednesday, and Saturday, and remarked that in his experience of opening Bodnant while he was in residence the visitors were not at all intrusive; since Aberconway was not recognized, he could wander the garden unmolested, and he thought they "improved" the garden. The suggestions in this letter were intended to ease Nancy out of a position of sole authority, although this could only be achieved with Lawrence's agreement, and to prepare him for the garden's remaining open while he was at Hidcote, since once the opening days were posted, they could not be changed to suit Johnston.

One can only commiserate with the Trust; Aberconway's letter demonstrates the problems created by having to constantly defer to Johnston's wishes. How much easier it would have been for them in those early days, when they were, after all, feeling their way in a new situation, to be able to take a decision as the need arose. But it seems that the Trust never once considered going behind Johnston's back: it kept his considerations very much in the forefront of all their dealings and was extremely careful never to step beyond the bounds of their responsibilities.

The garden was due to open in April 1949. In February, James Lees-Milne queried what arrangements, if any, had been made regarding this, pointing out that it would not be economical to have the gardeners

The Long Walk seen through one of the gazebos, c. 1973. Seymour Preston

"hanging about waiting for the public to come." Tickets would have to be provided, a notice posted (what would be the wording?), and perhaps a bell could be installed for visitors to pull to gain admittance (from the gardener on duty?). This last idea is faintly comical; the gardener could not be expected to busy himself within earshot of the bell three days a week.

Eventually, it was decided that "the gardens only will be open from April 1st to October 31st, Wednesday, Thursday and Saturday, from 2–5 P.M. at a fee of one shilling. For admittance please ring the bell." An attractive wooden sign with this painted message was prepared, and Mrs. Hughes, who had been appointed housekeeper for the manor, was assigned to collect the shillings, since her household duties, when Johnston was not there, were actually minimal.

Johnston had agreed to contribute to the running costs of Hidcote but up to the end of March 1949 had not paid anything. The Trust calculated that he owed £824, and was assured by Mr. Snelling, Johnston's accountant who held his power of attorney, that his client would reimburse the Trust eventually: "It's true that Lawrie Johnston's memory is going, but he is of the most scrupulous and honourable character."

The problem of money for Hidcote continued to vex the Trust, as did the question of the kitchen garden. Almost from the moment of the transfer, this enormous part of the garden had posed a problem. As Nancy Lindsay pointed out, the gardeners had grown masses of fruit and vegetables there during the war, and had been allowed a percentage of the profits by the Major. Afterward, however, he had been irritated by their inclination to concentrate on the kitchen garden rather than the flower garden and had intended to grass over at least half of the vegetable plots.

Then she informed them that Major Johnston, supposedly concerned lest Hidcote be turned into a commercial enterprise, and the gardeners distracted by the chance to earn a few extra shillings, did not want any produce at all to be sold, ever; not even the holly trimmings from the hedges that had previously been sold to local florists. This led to a confrontation between her and J. D. Inns, Johnston's land agent, who thought this was not her jurisdiction and furthermore threatened a source of revenue, however small. The correspondence over this matter, and the delicate politicking that it involved, widened the gulf of misunderstanding between Nancy and the Trust; in the end, the vegetables and holly continued to be sold.

Lord Aberconway, in his letter of November 1948, had suggested that the Trust would like to let the kitchen garden in part, retaining only the beds of old roses and peonies, and the greenhouses. This might have increased the income, but it was considered unwise. One day—and it was thought to be coming sooner rather than later—the Trust would be in the position of renting Hidcote Manor, and the fact of the kitchen garden being rented to another party might have prejudiced any prospects of future tenancy. So the year closed, the kitchen garden was maintained, and a small revenue was realized (£40). The Trust was beginning to look to the future.

Accounts for 1949, the first year of opening, showed that the money realized by renting the home farm to local farmers paid for little over half of the rates (the UK's property tax equivalent), tax, wages, and insurance; the £30 earned from admission fees had covered the cost of seed purchased; and with other expenses, Hidcote was running at a deficit of £1,650.

Five

THE HIDCOTE LESSON

After 1948 when he signed the Deed of Gift, Lawrence Johnston kept his English home and garden for another eight years, contrary to the National Trust's perennial assumption that the Major was not long for this world, and that it would soon be confronting the responsibility of renting out the manor while assuming total control of the garden and preparing it for public opening.

None of this occurred, however, until August 20, 1956, when Mr. Snelling, who held Johnston's power of attorney, notified the Trust that, "owing to the critically serious condition of health of the Major, there is no possibility whatsoever of his ever being able to reside at Hidcote again." The letter authorized the Trust to remove Johnston's effects to storage and to arrange for the rental or otherwise of the manor, as it deemed best.

Lawrence Johnston spent his final years at Serre de la Madone in the care of his valet, Albert Rebuffo. The gardener at the villa sold and gave away plants, and the health and appearance of the garden deteriorated along with Johnston's own: both, it appears with hindsight, were fading into the twilight of garden history. Like his mother, Lawrence suffered from paranoid delusions brought on by senile dementia. In particular, he began to doubt the honesty of one member of the Hidcote staff who had served him loyally for years; this behavior further isolated the old man.

Hidcote, with the Trust as a guardian, fared better. In 1951, the Trust had formed a local committee to oversee the maintenance of the gardens. Its members were Major Kenneth Shennan, Mrs. Heather Muir (of Kiftsgate), Mr. Joseph de Navarro (Mary de Navarro's son), and Lady Ismay. They had all known Hidcote in its heyday; Nancy Lindsay's direct involvement with Hidcote appears to have ended around this time.

The local committee was eventually to work hand in hand with Graham Stuart Thomas, who had recently been appointed as a Garden Adviser for the National Trust. In 1955, he reported that Hidcote was in danger of losing its position of preeminence, due to deterioration of the planting within the framework of hedges, which, fortunately, were still in first-class condition. In his opinion, the borders were in desperate need of reorganization and the trees and shrubs, which had been planted too closely together in the beginning, were now dangerously overcrowded. The Trust was obviously considering hiring a head gardener, and Thomas concurred, pointing out that although Albert Hawkins was devoted to the garden and knew all about the plants and their origins, he did not possess the broad base of knowledge that would make him capable of directing the work needed to reestablish the garden's finer qualities.

One year later, Major Shennan resigned his chairmanship of the local committee and the Trust decided to disband the group and put Graham Thomas in charge of Hidcote, with Heather Muir as codirector. When Thomas assumed responsibility for the garden, it was in a parlous state. He focused on retaining the best of Johnston's plants, while ripping out Hawkins's bedding that ran through the garden like a mindless refrain. Since the garden was to be a public showcase of good gardening, Thomas decided to increase the range of plants to provide a broader, color-filled display throughout the garden during its open months. (Thomas was known for his love and knowledge of old roses, and while Johnston had been among the few gardeners of his time to grow this group, Thomas found only about twenty different sorts, repeated through the garden; he enlarged the collection considerably.)

The house would be rented and it was decided that the tenant need not necessarily be a knowledgeable gardener, although this had at one time been considered a qualifying condition for a Hidcote tenant. In 1955, the Trust had received a letter from Pierrepont E. Johnson, Johnston's second cousin on his mother's side (the spelling of the family names does differ). Resident at Newport, Rhode Island, Johnson asked if the manor was available for rent, saying that he had last seen his cousin

A view of the main axis from the Old Garden, c. 1930. Jack Percival

The Circle remains a pivot point in the garden plan, c. 1930. Jack Percival

there in 1950, but knew that he was no longer directly involved with Hidcote. According to his nephew who visited Hidcote with his uncle, Pierrepont was a keen gardener who kept his family's estate near Boston in beautiful condition; in him the Trust might have found their dream tenant. Eventually, however, the property was let to Sir Gawain Bell, a retired British colonial administrator and diplomat and amateur artist.

On April 30, 1958, ten years after Lawrence Johnston transferred Hidcote to the National Trust, his solicitor wrote to its secretary informing them that Lawrence Johnston's funeral was to be held at Menton on May 3 and his body flown to England for burial at Mickleton according to the wishes expressed in his will. Johnston had died at Serre de la Madone on April 27 and was laid to rest next to his mother in Mickleton parish churchyard on May 14. He is identified as the son of Elliott Johnston and Gertrude Cleveland Winthrop by her first marriage, and as a GIFTED GARDENER AND HORTICULTURALIST, DEEPLY LOVED BY ALL HIS FRIENDS. *REQUIESCAT IN PACE.* The stones covering their graves bear the British lion rampant.

The Trust began the reclamation and modernization of the manor prior to renting, and at the end of October the executors held an auction of Johnston's effects. This included Jacobean and Queen Anne furniture, Sèvres and Dresden porcelain, and nearly five hundred books. It can be safely assumed that this collection included many volumes on gardening by the eminent authors of Johnston's day, including E. A. Bowles and Ellen Willmott, who were also friends of the Major; Miss Willmott at one time gave Johnston a plant of the beautiful, and at that time rare, *Clematis florida* 'Sieboldii,' while Bowles once described Johnston as having come to England to play in a tennis tournament but lost both the match and his heart to that country. It will be painful for modern bibliophiles and collectors of garden literature to know that Lawrence's books realized a grand total of nearly £7.

Work in the garden in the three years since Graham Thomas's initial report had done much to improve its appearance. So successful was the Trust that one lady, Mrs. Fleischmann, who had "known the garden well in the height of its glory," wrote to congratulate the Trust:

> The clearing or thinning out has left no blemish even of a temporary nature.
> The lovely vista from the little green garden [Mrs. Winthrop's Garden] is

quite restored . . . three-quarters of [the Stream Garden] has been cleared of rubbish with much replanting of primulas. . . . ringing of a row of apples in the kitchen garden at the back of the old roses enables you to see the collection of lilacs in front of the apple orchard . . . [and the] unusual collection of single peonies in perfection. . . .

She concluded that she found "the whole place most beautifully cared for."

But despite this apparent success, and the appointment of a new board as Hidcote's caretakers, its transition from private home to public asset muddled along. The new administrative board consisted of some very strong personalities, and almost inevitably they came to verbal if not physical blows, with Alvilde Lees-Milne (whose husband James Lees-Milne had been instrumental in securing Hidcote for the Trust) opposing Graham Stuart Thomas on most things concerning the garden. The committee members squabbled with each other as, in Thomas's opinion, each individual thought he or she knew what was the best course of

One of the ornaments surviving the dispersal of Johnston's collection, c. 1970. Seymour Preston

action for Hidcote, so they struggled to maintain Hidcote, making decisions that were often misguided (for example, putting Albert Hawkins in charge of the gardeners—Hawkins had been in charge of the vegetable garden and as Johnston had forecast, did not have the respect of the other gardeners, who ignored his orders). One particularly touchy moment, which divided the board once again, involved the Trust's purchase of a monument to honor Lawrence Johnston—James Lees-Milne added his caustic opinion that far from being a fitting memorial to Johnston's genius and generosity in leaving Hidcote to the nation, the chosen urn was shoddy and the gesture as hollow as the urn. Thomas, meanwhile, argued that gardening by committee did not serve the garden well and found it extremely frustrating to watch the garden deteriorate as a result.

Nevertheless, and despite all the bickering and internal disagreements, with what it achieved at Hidcote, the National Trust really came into its own as a custodian of fine gardens. In 1958, to mark the tenth anniversary of the acquisition of Hidcote, a new guidebook was prepared, and Vita Sackville-West was invited to contribute the introduction. When she accepted the commission, she had not visited Hidcote for a good many years, and Graham Thomas offered to give her a guided tour so that her description could be as fresh as the garden. But her piece appeared as an adaptation of the article she first wrote in 1949 for the *Journal of the Royal Horticultural Society.* At the time she was writing, the Trust was eager to boost admissions, and Sackville-West closed the article by expressing "the hope that gardeners and garden-lovers will visit Hidcote in their thousands." She may have been thinking of the "shillingses" (a name she invented for visitors referring to the cost of admission to her garden) that she hoped would come to visit her own garden, Sissinghurst, but her wishes for Hidcote have been more than fulfilled. Today over 100,000 people from all walks of life and from all over the world visit Hidcote each year.

Such popularity has not been without its problems. There are, as Glyn Jones puts it, "Two sides to the National Trust coin: enterprise and conservation." For the latter, the National Trust is obligated to maintain the continuity of its properties by holding to the inspiration of the original owners. This is less difficult to achieve in cases where one family has been the sole custodian for several centuries and documentation and family archives help to guide the development of a working program, but in the case of a garden like Hidcote, the life work of one man, who left no records and whose traditions were preserved only in the memories of those who once worked for him, the management program can only be based on research and, to some degree, informed supposition. Hidcote has been compared unfavorably to Sissinghurst. It, too, belongs to the National Trust, but with that garden came a well-documented history and profile of its makers; their likes and dislikes, experiments and firmly held beliefs were recorded in diaries and countless articles in newspapers, magazines, and radio broadcasts. Sissinghurst had been gardened by the Nicolsons almost to the moment the Trust took it on, and then by gardeners who had actually worked with its creators and so had firsthand knowledge of their aesthetic and vision for the place.

Hidcote, on the other hand, was in 1958 functionally an orphan of nearly fifteen years' standing; Johnston's direct involvment had receded, but his expressed desire to remain in charge had tied the Trust's hands during the early years. When at last the Trust was able to install its own head gardener, "Harry" Burrows, he had only the memories of several elderly gardeners to educate him and the Trust in Johnston's ways in the rehabilitation of a garden that had been at its peak almost thirty years before.

Then there is the Trust's other obligation, to the visiting public. As road conditions improved and the numbers of car-owning families spending their extended leisure time visiting country houses and gardens increased, so did admissions. Each generation has been able to travel farther more readily, while garden appreciation tours have become big business, and to remain profitable more open days are added to the calendar and more events scheduled to entice the public and boost revenues. The result, for a property like Hidcote and, indeed, for the many others like it that were originally made for the solitary pleasure of one person who occasionally admitted close friends or select small groups, has been not only an enlargement of visitors' facilities that encroach on the garden picture, but also a loss of the sense of the garden's repose; the air of graceful serenity that was as much a part of a gentleman's estate as the trees and flowers, is easily obliterated by the sheer weight of numbers admitted.

A concomitant of this is the damaging effect that visitor traffic has on the very fabric of a garden. Johnston, in spite of his relative wealth, could not lavish vast sums on the construction of the garden. Pathways and staircases were not made on stable foundations and began crumbling; traditional skills and materials were not as readily available and were expensive if secured, so modern repairs were made that often jar with the obvious age of the garden.

Although garden history today is a mainstream academic subject, not so long ago it was, as a scholarly discipline, relatively new, and its methodologies are a fairly recent invention. However, considering the importance of Hidcote to the history of English garden design, it is surprising that so little serious effort was expended until quite recently documenting its creation and the life of Lawrence Johnston. It was realized quite early on that there were no written records (it being assumed, on the strength of a supposition by James Lees-Milne, that Nancy Lindsay had burned them up in a fit of pique at not inheriting Hidcote), and in those early days there were enough people left who knew Johnston who could have provided an oral history, which if anything is more valuable than a written record. But even the collection of oral history has become a scholarly subject; so that now when the Trust documents a property it does so within a framework of tested practice. In the 1970s, when Seymour Preston and his wife were visitors at Hidcote and he began interviewing and writing to Johnston's remaining friends, he was actually laying down a frame of reference. Sadly, the Trust was less than supportive, and Preston's final manuscript was dismissed as a trivial effort rather than as a door opening onto the past.

When it came to researching for the first edition of this book, the Trust was more forthcoming and assisted me to the best of its ability—and mine, which I might add has increased with the years—yet when I look back at that time the phrase that sticks in my mind, uttered by one of the Hidcote gardeners, which one I can't recall, is that Hidcote was the Cinderella of the Trust properties. There was no record from which a "mission statement" for the garden might have evolved, which in turn would have aided the garden staff in their work so that they might have felt less demoralized. David Owen, assistant head gardener in the 1990s, was the first Trust employee to undertake systematic historical research. In 1999, the garden historian Katie Fretwell became involved in researching the garden's history and with that the Trust began to reevaluate its care of Hidcote and take steps to improve the situation. And this goes back to the

Trust's lack of experience in the field of garden conservation and an unwillingness, perhaps, to expend the energy and funds needed to preserve a twentieth-century garden when there were far more historic and, by that token, valuable properties needing attention.

By the late 1980s, however, the attitude changed. Dr. Peter Goodchild at Kings Manor, University of York, was leading the way in the methodology of garden history, and by the late 1990s, Katie Fretwell wrote, "every National Trust property—whether a house, garden, workhouse, or park—should have at least a basic archive with copies of the main historical sources." One can only say, "Not a minute too soon." Over the years, the Trust has become a proving ground for garden research and recording techniques. Hidcote, in effect, put them in this position, so it can be said that the garden, which was seminal to the development of twentieth-century English garden design, was among those that established the modern practice and study of garden conservation.

We can only be grateful that the Trust realized that unless serious steps were taken Hidcote would vanish, but major programs of renovation take major funding and in this the Trust was lucky: at the turn of the twenty-first century, an anonymous American donor stepped forward. Claiming kinship to Johnston's family, the donor enabled the first round of garden restoration projects, including returning the garden's entrance to the original site, across the front of the manor and under the great cedar of Lebanon. This donor has committed further gifts to the Hidcote fund on the understanding that the National Trust must contribute matching sums, so a dedicated fund-raiser was added to the Hidcote staff.

As a result, substantial improvements are underway throughout the garden. For example, beds entirely planted with iris or peony as Johnston had them make a breathtaking show, but, the Trust reasoned, are over in the blink of an eye, leaving behind an uninspiring thicket of foliage. Furthermore, the man-hours needed to maintain such a brief show of limited attraction could be better spent on plantings that provide permanent display, and finally, visitors have been conditioned to expect year-round color and excitement in all parts of a public garden. At Hidcote, attempts were made early on to cater to this expectation. New thinking, however, has changed all that.

Consequently, peonies, which were the main feature of the Pillar
Garden, had previously been spread around the garden, but are now
given a renewed presence in the Pillar Garden, where a collection of
Mouton tree peonies has also been developed. The Summer House (now
called the Plant House), which was sited along the northern edge of the
Lily Pool, was taken down some years ago; dilapidated, it was deemed
more efficient to demolish it than to restore it. But it was a great loss, as
the bed that took its place never held the same attraction as the original
collection of exotica that once filled the Plant House. So among the
many restoration projects throughout the garden, the return of the Plant
House has been a great success, reminding visitors that Johnston was,
first and foremost, a plant collector, who selected plants not just for their
rarity, but also for their beauty and their scent, which was evidently one

The Summer House (now the Plant
House) in its original state before it fell
derelict and was demolished by the
National Trust.

of Johnston's prime criteria for a good plant. Hidcote is one of the most fragrant gardens, and its many little rooms are just what the Elizabethan philosopher Francis Bacon recommended in his essay "On Gardens"— that enclosures be made throughout the garden where the perfume of flowers can be captured for pleasure.

Johnston had a collection of urns and tubs scattered throughout the garden, all planted to mimic vases of flowers. There was also much statuary, and numerous conversation groups of Regency garden furniture graced the terraces and lawns. Many of these pieces were dispersed early on to other Trust properties—perhaps it was thought to be impractical to have these valuable pieces cluttering up the small garden rooms, risking damage by visitors. However, their loss detracts from the character of the garden, and so the Hidcote staff is working to track down and restore as many of these items as possible to their proper home in the garden.

The Summer House, c. 1930. Jack Percival

The newly reinstated Plant House, one of the main projects undertaken by the National Trust to return Hidcote Manor Gardens to its appearance in the 1930s, when the garden had reached its maturity but before it began its decline. Andrea Jones

Inevitably, nature caused the greatest alterations. In the 1970s, Dutch elm disease obliterated the avenue of Huntingdon elms. A sizable *Cupressus macrocarpa* that grew at the northwest corner of the Pillar Garden came down in a storm; one of the great beech trees that formed the pair on the raised dais at the western end of the Theatre Lawn died, and the tall trees encircling the lawn in murky mystery have vanished—as have the days when Lady Diana Manners would *jeté* onto the lawn in a flutter of pale silk veils against the dark hedges. Yet all these depredations have had an up side and have allowed old garden features to be reinstated.

Gardens by their very nature are creatures of change, and we know that Johnston was ever ready to try something new. It has long been the Trust's and Glyn Jones's avowed purpose to respect the "ethos" of the garden. However, earlier management decisions were less informed than they are today. For example, the rockery that runs along the base of the Stilt Garden platform was turned into a cistus bank when its shading structure was dismantled. Although the cistus—planted with a wide variety of Mediterranean shrubs—was ideally suited to the free-draining soil

A sequence of photos showing the demise of the Huntingdon elm avenue and its replanting from 1973 to 1979.

Seymour Preston

and produced an overall pleasing effect, recalling Johnston's lifelong connections with the south of France, it was not what Johnston had intended. The original scheme for the site is best known from the history, oral and written, related by Jack Percival, who as a teenager came to work at Hidcote.

Jack first wrote to me in 1991, briefly describing his work at Hidcote and regretting that we had not been in touch for the first edition of my book, as, he told me, he would "love to have been in it." Jack deserves his

The avenue in 2008, replanted with beech. This stately avenue is, in effect, an iteration of the yew-lined Long Walk, contrasting its informal, woodland atmosphere with the elegant formality of the mown grass promenade. Andrea Jones

The Theatre Lawn, c. 1988. Johnston favored these unardorned interludes in the Hidcote plan to give contrast as well as restful moments. Seymour Preston

place in this edition since his memories of Hidcote have guided much of the restoration and replanting that have taken place. Glyn Jones, who has been at Hidcote since 1998, has the greatest respect for Jack, having learned that even though Jack was just a teenager and Hidcote was his first job, his memory, some six decades later, of all that happened was sharp and accurate. I, too, recall with fondness Jack's friendly willingness to help me (he went through the book page by page, commenting and correcting where he could). I offer these quotes from Jack's letters to me as evidence of the sort of man he was and what the making of Hidcote involved. (I have corrected some spelling and punctuation for clarity.)

28 April 91
I was employed at Hidcote in 1930 until 1934–35 under the Head Mr. Adams & lodged with Charlie Frensham before he left for Serre de La Madone. I took over from a young man who had gone out to the French garden earlier. He was called Harold Branch.

I worked with all the men you have mentioned in your book, they were my personal friends, and I can name you some more who worked in the gar-

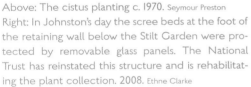

Above: The cistus planting c. 1970. Seymour Preston
Right: In Johnston's day the scree beds at the foot of
the retaining wall below the Stilt Garden were pro-
tected by removable glass panels. The National
Trust has reinstated this structure and is rehabilitat-
ing the plant collection. 2008. Ethne Clarke

dens during my time. Mark Stanley who had worked for the Hanburys in
La Mortola came & took Charlie Frensham's position.

My work was on the rockeries, lime free border, old garden border &
border back of stilt garden etc. . . . I knew Mr. & Mrs. Merrill they were
very kind, as after all I was only 16 at the time, it was my first position away
from home. My Father obtained me the situation as he knew Mr. Adams &
Hidcote, He, my father, being Head Gardener to Blathwayts of Porlock
[who were] also great gardeners & friends of the Major and paid a visit to
Hidcote during my term there.

24 May 1991
With reference to the Lime free beds at Hidcote, I was in on that job [in]
1933 with Ted Pearce, Walt Bennett, & Albert Hawkins; the beds were dug
out to 3 feet deep and lorry loads of very old sawdust from timber yards at
Blockley, & Railway ashes & clinkers from Campden station were brought
to the kitchen garden area, and we had to wheel all this material to the

A view from the Lower Stream Garden, c. 1988, looking though the tree canopy; such views were kept open in Johnston's time. Ethne Clarke

In the Upper Stream Garden, c. 2008, *Lysimachia punctata* or skunk cabbage and Siberian irises are among the many water-loving and marginal plants that obscure the tiny water course. Ethne Clarke

stream area of the garden, it took several weeks hard work! [*Jack made a point later of explaining to me that the wheelbarrows themselves were incredibly heavy with iron wheels and heavy boarding for sides. And it was often raining while they worked. —EC*]

27 Oct 1995

[In] 1932 Hidcote had a frame-yard where a lot of frames were made from railway sleepers [ties], & many filled with coarse sand; all the pots of seeds were in 6 inch pots & then plunged and covered with asbestos covers, and all the watering was done overhead until germination, this was a job I had to look after, the seedlings [were next] put up on a large tray-like structure of coarse sand & again plunged but covered by the old "Chase" cloches, later to be pinched out and sent to various places.

. . . Given to me when I started at Hidcote was a notebook full of numbers down left of each page, and each had a name of a plant or shrub of some kind [against it]. [*Some of these labels corresponding to the notebook numbers were still in place in the garden in the late 1990s. —EC*]

When I was at Hidcote in 1933 the second half of Westonbirt was developed, and most of the trees, shrubs and ground cover at that time came from Marchants Nurseries at Wimborne in Dorset. Yes, besides the flamingos were two pairs of Gold Pheasants, and an Ostrich & that was enough; it took five or six of the garden employees to catch this bird to put it away in the winter quarters, and it had a kick like a mule if you were unlucky.

The beds in the old garden were always very full indeed of many varieties of plants & you mention many. The Dahlia is mentioned but not to the extent that it was used. These same beds were even planted up for summer with many varieties of Dahlias, one I have always remembered was Jersey Beauty, a lovely pale pink (now where the present National Trust shop is that was a block of four loose boxes or stables, very strongly made to take strong farm horses). Well it was in here that all the Dahlias were stored for winter under a deep covering of straw from the frame, one other item I remember is that the names of the tubers in each loose box were written on the woodwork. Alas, too late.

As one walked from the Theatre Lawn past the Camellia shelter we had another small greenhouse which housed a large collection of nerines, none must be watered from the top, (this came under my charge) a cement trough was made and the bulbs as they became dry would be stood for a while in the water then returned to the staging.

11 November 1995

When one day after I had been at Hidcote around shall we say some 6 months, Mr. Adams said just out of the blue, "How are you progressing with names of plants? I will be asking you one day." And so that day came, in the frame yard. "What is the name of that plant? Hesitation, Don't know sir."

"What do you mean 'don't know'? In the time you have been here, it's time you knew. I will give you just another chance, and if you don't know then, you can pack your bags & "B" well get off home & I will "B" well write & tell your Father why you have "B" well been sent home. So get your "B" self together and "B" well know the next time I ask you." "Yes Sir!"

So as it happened I was on greenhouse duty & fires that evening so took the plant label into the stoke-hole with me & with the light from Hurricane lantern wrote the name down & went back to my lodging & by the morning knew the name, but of course I was not asked for around another

The Maple Garden, shown here in 2008, has been replanted to recall its look in Johnston's day. This is probably the first garden area worked by Johnston, and his mother may well have taken a hand in its planting. Andrea Jones

The Old Garden, shown here in 2008, is one of the areas nearest the house. Formal in layout, this large area is informally planted with old-fashioned roses and perennials. The paving of broken slabs supports the relaxed feel of this garden area and may offer evidence of Johnston's attempts to economize. Andrew Lawson

three weeks. When it was, "Well young Jack, what is the name of the plant I asked you, do you know?" "Yes sir. ARGYROXIPHIUM SANDWICENSIS VAR MACROCEPHYLUM." "Good for you!" And it has stayed with me all my life . . . from then on life became very comfortable & I never had any more sticky moments.

In 1988, Graham Thomas remembered how, when he arrived on the Hidcote scene, Westonbirt was choked with mildewed berberis. These were grubbed up and replaced by species roses, thickets of cotoneaster, and stands of birch trees. The hips and berries were meant to add autumn color and show off against the bark of a wide range of trees, but also to provide winter food for the birds that inhabit the woodland, recalling the time when it was home for the more exotic inhabitants of Johnston's aviary. Today, Westonbirt is again in need of attention and is on the priority list for the Hidcote garden team. But whether or not the birds are returned remains a question. In a 1904 *Country Life* story on Sutton

Courtenay Manor, the author remarks, "The Lord of the Manor [Harry Lindsay] is an enthusiastic ornithologist and has made a bird sanctuary of the grounds not for collecting but for preserving wild life. The idea is a very beautiful one and will be followed by an increasing number of people in various parts of the country." Lindsay's friend and neighbor, Lawrence Johnston was one of these people—and he installed a sanctuary at Serre de la Madone, too. But today's caretakers, when weighing up the pros and cons of putting birds back into Hidcote, would do well to remember Jack Percival's lament about having to wrestle the ostrich into its quarters.

Although Nancy Lindsay's direct involvement with Hidcote ended during the early 1950s, she inherited Serre de la Madone from Lawrence. Lawrence had originally left the villa and money he had in a Monte Carlo bank to Norah but on her death had switched the inheritance to Nancy. (The earlier-mentioned Ruth Peppercorn had also been considered as a possible heiress for this garden.) Sadly, in spite of the bequest, Nancy— whose main source of income was, she claimed, taking commissions to paint architectural portraits of houses, which kept her from the plants she loved—recognized that she did not have the funds to maintain the estate, and sold the villa. However, with her eye on the plant collections as a transferable asset, she invited the Cambridge University Botanic Garden to take whatever plants, seeds, or propagating material they wished as a living memorial to Lawrence Johnston and his student days at Cambridge. In 1959, the university received two groups of plants, but by 1985 few remained of the many received: the list compiled that year by the Botanic Garden gives five mahonia species, including *Mahonia* × *lindsayae* 'Cantab' and four others (*M. lomariifolia* was first introduced at Hidcote by Lawrence Johnston), a red-leaved form of *Phormium tenax,* white-flowered *Amaryllis belladonna, Sarcococca ruscifolia,* and *Osmanthus* × *fortunei.*

Throughout her life, Nancy nursed a proprietariness to all things Hidcote, as well as any plant she had touched, believing that she retained some degree of ownership. So this entitled her to use the Cambridge collection as a source of propagating material (a ploy she also exercised with plants at Hidcote, and those collected by her during expeditions to Persia; some of these were also grown at Kew). A decade or more of plant-swapping and seed exchanges between Nancy and Kew is revealed in letters between her and the curator; Nancy "coveting" many of their plants and offering Kew choice items in return, including plants from Hidcote, such as a double-flowered daphne. Graham Stuart Thomas remembered obtaining 'Rose d'Hivers' via Kew from Nancy's collection; Nancy called it "the darling of my heart" and in a letter to Thomas explained her dismay—"more than even my placid nature can stand"—that Kew had "given" it to someone else before she even had any in stock for herself. To make amends, she proposed that Thomas share with her any stock he raised, fifty-fifty.

In spite of her difficulties (the ones she created for herself, financial and personal, and the ones she made for others), Nancy deserved a degree of respect as an able plantswoman, and the lists she compiled of the plants available from her garden and nursery at Manor Cottage, Sutton Courtenay, at Abingdon in Berkshire, are breathtaking. Thomas wrote that "few people had a better 'eye' for a good plant, or guarded it more tenaciously when they had acquired it."

Her masterpiece, by far, is the Shrub Rose List. Here are all the roses that she would have known from Hidcote, plus many more, including ones she introduced herself. The descriptions of the roses help to explain Nancy's practice lists of adjectives, like the ones compiled in her Persian notebooks.

> 'Kazanlik' The Turkish attar-of-roses, sent from Constantinople over 40 years ago to my beautiful young mother, has cascades of ambrosial, pellucid rose-pink flowers with lambent coral hearts, over jungles of mint green.

> 'Rose d'Hivers' L. 1409 [indicating one of Nancy's collection] From Bavavali of the Lurs high in the Elburz Mts . . . exquisitely made 'cabbages' of dawn pink shaded malmaison. The Luris women gather nosegays in high summer which preserved in vases of faience mature to a rich rose-du-Barry spicily fragrant all winter long.

'Gloire de Guilan,' 'Sharastanek,' and the wonderful 'Rose de Resht' with flowers of "pigeons-blood ruby irised with royal purple" also bear Nancy's identifying numbers.

"Rose de Resht," shown here in 2008. One of Nancy Lindsay's collections from Persia, it was a splendid addition to the catalogue of old-fashioned roses prized by her and her mother, Norah Lindsay. Today, it retains its popularity in the heritage rose category.
Andrew Lawson

"'Hidcote Gold' brought from the Yunnan by Major Johnston in the 1930s, a gigantic briar," "'Lawrence Johnston' a graceful climber," and "'Souvenir de Norah Lindsay'" recall the partnership that gave Nancy her calling. The description of her mother's rose is revealing:

> A glorious scion of 'La France' and 'Spanish Beauty'; a statuesque shrub with dragon-barbed mahogany canes flaunting beautiful, shining emerald leaves, and clusters of several very great single chalices with wide glistening petals, flamingo-pink within, cochineal without, and flashing sunbursts of rich gold at their hearts, sweetly fragrant. The massive vermillion lacquer hips endure often all winter.

At one time, Nancy listed more than one dozen varieties of peony, two dozen named irises, many introduced by Basil Leng from his gardens in the south of France; nine bergenias, sixteen geraniums and an equal number of hostas, eight euphorbias, and nearly a dozen sedums. All of these are signature plants at Hidcote.

Through Nancy's involvement, during the late 1950s and '60s, with gardens like New College, Oxford, where she helped John Buxton with the replanting and improvement of the herbaceous border, and Summer Fields, a private school also at Oxford, and through her advice to budding gardeners like Rosemary Verey, who credited Nancy with teaching her about "layered" planting, using groundcovers like perennial geraniums and periwinkle as a matrix through which choicer plants could emerge in season, the Hidcote style was brought into the gardens of the late twentieth century.

There is much the owner of even the smallest garden can learn from Hidcote, most obviously because of the way the ten-acre garden is divided into small gardens, each with its own character, any of which could be translated to a contemporary residential garden. In fact, celebrating Hidcote's century anniversary in 2007, the garden designer Chris Beardshaw created a show garden for the RHS Chelsea Flower Show that featured plants raised by the Hidcote gardeners. Using a Hidcote-style gazebo as a focal point, Beardshaw translated the hedged enclosures and ebullient, color-themed planting into a design that could be easily realized in a rectangular plot of land, big or small.

But at Hidcote the themes that stand out include Mrs. Winthrop's blue and green patio garden; the Cottage Garden filled with plants that grow to head height; hedges of the old striped gallica 'Rosa Mundi,' or the renowned patchwork hedges of holly, hornbeam, yew, and box. The notions are seemingly endless.

By far one of the best lessons to be learned is the importance of good foliage plants: plants that add to the garden picture before and after their flowering period. Hidcote shows that there are many shades of green, and that tints of yellow and brown are integral parts of an artist's palette. Also, texture and form allied with subtle shading can often hold the eye more comfortably than carefully planned rainbow borders. It was Johnston's genius to understand all the aspects of his plant material and to extend its use beyond the "cheerful show" that was normally expected of it.

Finally, when visiting Hidcote remember that the garden was the vision of one man, made for the enjoyment of his friends and for his own personal satisfaction, and that in many ways it still reflects his enthusiasms and preferences. The most important thing we can learn from Major Johnston is to have confidence in our own instincts. To be inspired by trends and informed by gardening gurus is one thing; to follow them slavishly is another.

In 2000, when Hidcote visitor numbers hit 100,000 for the first time, the garden became self-financing. Glyn Jones, as head gardener, started a program of revitalization that impacted not just the fabric of the garden, but the gardeners themselves, instituting a modern management style (one of the gardeners calls it "laid back") along with an intelligent use of modern equipment—like electrical outlets, which are now installed in key areas throughout the garden so that power equipment cords no longer have to be dragged hundreds of feet to prune a hedge (and there are hundreds of feet of hedges!).

Significantly, Jones recognizes that it is the individual touch of inspiration that instills a garden with life. Now, rather than gardening by committee, with the head gardener serving as the "man of all work" as the previous head gardener had struggled for some twenty-plus years, Jones heads a staff of senior gardeners, each of whom has his or her own team, with each assigned an area of the garden as their own. Keeping in mind the Trust's dictum to maintain Hidcote according to Johnston's "ethos," these skilled individuals are given the latitude to plant and care for their areas as they deem appropriate. This, says Jones, allows them an all-important sense of ownership in the garden.

In 2001, Mike Beeston joined as property manager, a job that had fallen on the previous head gardener's shoulders. Now those diverse tasks are handled by another team, leaving the full-time gardeners time to garden. Volunteers, too, are now welcome in the garden, bringing the workforce closer to the number of gardeners Johnston employed (and had supplemented with farmworkers during busy times).

In 2002, with money to fund the first five-year restoration plan, the team began by replacing some of Hidcote's smaller but more telling features, such as the circular seat on the Cedar Lawn surrounding the base of the great tree that anchors the entire scheme. Important structures that had been removed were replaced: most significantly the Plant House near the

Lily Pool. Replanting occurred in the Pillar Garden (more and better peonies, plus tapering 'Amanogowa' cherries whose shape mimics the yew topiary pillars). Says Jones, "Colleagues come by and give me a lot of trouble for planting these trees that are now so unfashionable, but these are what Johnston would have known and used. And that is the point." And with a carpet of peonies, aquilegias, alliums, and poppies spread beneath their powder-puff blossom-laden branches, it's a look I could easily learn to love.

These are just a few of the features Jones pointed out to me as we walked the garden together one day in May 2008, and are the ones which stand out as true points of difference between the old Hidcote and the new. To begin with, the new management plan covers the next 150 years, climate change, and economic issues (like planting a shelterbelt of beech trees to succeed the existing woodland as it thins, and augmenting it with a cash crop of pines). The fact that there are long-range management plans at all is significant.

A period color photo by Archie Renfrew, showing that the White Garden was at one time planted with mauve and blue phlox, has inspired the gardeners to repeat the scheme, using phlox selected from varieties that will have been trialed at Hidcote. This brings together the past and future, recalling Johnston's practice of always selecting the best, while at the same time making Hidcote relevant to contemporary plant breeding programs.

Hidcote is a botanical repository of live specimens, and a grafting program has been initiated to preserve historic varieties of as yet unidentified shrubby plants and trees, like heritage apples in the orchard and old roses from the rose walk.

The 2-D side of Johnston's creative pursuits is being brought into focus as the maquette that he painted of his garden has finally been found—in the attic of another Trust property. It is being restored and when the manor house opens to the public for the first time in 2009, will be part of an interpretive display on the ground floor, from where visitors will once again be able to enter the garden. (This painting, Johnston's own interpretation of his garden, served as the reference for the jacket artwork of this book—complete with his spaniel Timmy rollicking across the grass walk.)

In 2005, the next round of renovations was funded, including the most significant restoration of the Rock Bank. In creating this anew, the original water pipes and taps were unearthed as well as the "snowmelt" pools that fed the little recirculating stream that ran along its western edge. This water feature is being put back, too.

Looking forward, Jones hopes to find a suitable replacement for the less-than-attractive tar macadam path in the Rose Walk. But the most significant change, and one that was not necessarily due to a major injection of money, was the reinstatement of the entrance to the garden from the house, below the cedar of Lebanon. As I wrote earlier, entering the garden from the courtyard across the front of the Great Lawn threw visitors into the middle of the main vista, from which point it was hard to get a bearing on the plan. Now the long sweep of the grass walk between the Cedar Lawn and the twin gazebos is seen in an uninterrupted view, tak-

In the Pillar Garden, 2008, spots of bright orange from annual poppy flowers remind visitors that it was Johnston's favorite color—a sunny, gregarious choice for such a shy, reclusive man. Andrew Lawson

The National Trust recently reinstated the Rock Bank and will be returning the small water feature running along the foot of the bank, which is intended to resemble the running water of a snow-melt stream, 2008. Andrew Lawson

ing in The Circle, the Red Borders, and the Stilt Garden, leading the eye to the gates framing the distant view of the Vale of Evesham. This glimpse of the outside world from within the confines of the private world of Hidcote is what leads you on, discovering, as you advance, all the joys and secrets that Johnston so carefully fashioned. It is, in every sense, a work of art.

THE GARDEN IN SEASON

"Hidcote is not a single-season place. If it is richest in summer, it is most delicately precious in spring. It is full of arresting effects in autumn, while the beauty of form is most obvious in winter, when riot of growth does not obscure that placid quality."

—H. Avary Tipping, *Country Life*, February 1930, page 244

Notes from my visits in the mid-to-late 1980s were the source for the following paragraphs. This being a National Trust garden where continuity is the benchmark, I discovered during visits between 1998 and 2008 that little had changed as far as main planting schemes were concerned, so if used alongside the current garden guide it's a useful tool, suggesting what has changed and what has remained the same. I have done this myself using Anna Pavord's own seasonal break-down of the garden, from *Hidcote: The Garden and Lawrence Johnston*. What has changed is the circumstance surrounding the care and maintenance of this most historic English garden. No longer the Cinderella of the Trust's family, Hidcote has had the glass slipper fitted to it by its donor, who, as mentioned, charged the National Trust to meet his donated sums with matching funds.

Spring

In late April, the garden is just beginning to shake off its winter mantle. The beech hedges, the hornbeam allées, and the Stilt Garden have to yet to break into leaf, so their framework is easily studied. The short arbor that forms the eastern boundary of Mrs. Winthrop's Garden resembles the prow of an overturned ship, and through its ribs can be seen the golden carpet of *Lysimachia punctata* and doronicum, which are the first hints of this small garden's blue and gold scheme.

The beds here and in the Red Borders are tufted with emerging foliage, but at the far end of the Stilt Garden the plantings of yellow-belled *Fritillaria imperialis* are in full bloom and draw the eye to the famous view through the decorative wrought-iron gates.

The beds of the Old Garden contain many early bulbs, particularly in the south borders. There, at the foot of a north-facing wall, in the specially prepared lime-free beds, clusters of erythronium, *Anemone blanda*, and hellebores add their muted flower tints to the opening colors of rhododendron and azalea.

Mrs. Winthrop's Garden devoid of the ornament, sundial, and other features Johnston lavished on this small space, c. 1988. Ethne Clarke

Mrs. Winthrop's Garden has been repopulated with a sundial and tropical-filled urns to accent the Mediterranean feel of the space. 2008. Andrew Lawson.

The new growth dusts the box topiary hens and low edging in the White Garden with fresh green, and a few white tulips inaugurate the color theme, as the beds of the Maple Garden await their fill of seasonal annuals.

Perhaps the most satisfying section of the garden this early in the season is the Stream Garden. Later in the year, its foliage is so dense and the canopy of trees so enveloping that the sense of "depth" is hard to appreciate. From here, the lowest point of the garden, it is possible to understand the topography of Hidcote and the ingenuity of Johnston in dealing with it.

Standing on the path and looking north back toward Mrs. Winthrop's Garden, you will notice the drop in the level of the hedges that defines the contours of the terracing. Continue along the path and across the broad grass avenue, then stop where the stream path continues. The Stream Garden continues to fall away from you, eventually trailing off into the pastoral scene of fields and farm buildings beyond.

There is a curious rhythm about the four main vistas at Hidcote; two of them, from the Stream Garden and from Mrs. Winthrop's, are both

(above, right, and opposite) Main axes at Hidcote, 2008: from the Stilt Garden looking toward the manor house; the view through one of the gazebos down the Long Walk; and the view midway down the Long Walk showing the sunken Stream Garden crossing it. Right: Andrea Jones, Opposite: Ethne Clarke

worthy of Claude Lorrain or Poussin, whose artistic formulae for the portrayal of natural landscape informed the garden design of the Landscape Movement. The other two vistas, both best seen from the vantage point of the twin gazebos, adhere strictly to the classical idea of viewing the distant landscape from within the formal framework of the well-ordered garden.

From the vantage point of The Circle, the grassy rondel, it is worth considering the symmetry of the garden picture looking toward the Stilt Garden. The precision of the planes within the receding perspective is eerily mathematical. And again, Johnston's notion of a wild garden within a formal setting establishes a rhythmical alternation of tonsured shrub and pollarded tree with subjects left to follow their natural inclination.

The Stream Garden banks perfectly demonstrate the value of good foliage. *Lysichitum americanum*, the bog arum, is beginning to unfurl its huge, shiny green leaves around the brassy yellow Easter lily–shaped flowers, and all around, mass plantings, of *Brunnera macrophylla*, *Symphytum grandiflorum*, astrantia, and astilbe, contribute a wide variety of leaf shape, texture, and tint. Elsewhere along the stream, groupings of

Pachysandra terminalis, Tellima grandiflora, and geranium species creep along beneath uncurling fern fronds. This is ground cover at its best, and it is fascinating to study the progression of this garden area over the year.

Summer

Mid-May, and Hidcote Manor Garden is coloring up: the famous hedges in particular are best seen now, for the freshness of mahogany-purple beech and lime-green corrugated hornbeam foliage is to the forefront. Looking from The Circle toward the filigree gate, the copper beech hedge nearest contrasts with the green boxes atop the Stilts, and both fresh colors are offset against the dustiness of the mop-headed holm oaks towering either side of the gate.

The copper beech here complements the pale mauve of Rouen lilacs, *Syringa chinensis,* and the underplanting of hellebore species and *Alchemilla conjuncta.*

Lilacs are a specialty of Hidcote, and in May the Rose Walk is perfumed by a collection of nearly thirty different varieties and species. The lilacs grow up between the pillars of Irish yew stationed along both sides of the walk. Beneath the lilacs, the rose-bush foliage billows, and heads of *Allium aflatunense,* purple, flowered auriculas and repeat edge planting of purple sage bring the color of the lilac blossom to the lower levels of the border. Grey-leaved foliage plants are used to complement and lighten the soft mauves: *Helichrysum lanatum* and clumps of dianthus and santolina appear at regular intervals in the foreground. Swaths of woolly symphytum foliage contrast against glistening leathery bergenia leaves on the orchard side of the border with the emerging foliage of peony and hemerocallis that hints at the continuing display.

Standing at the south end of the Rose Walk, beneath the *Robinia* x *ambigua* 'Decaisneana' that marks the head of the path, one looks down the dingy walk to a bright white-painted iron bench. The planting at this end of the border and around the little bench is worth recording. The seat is framed by equally bright plantings of white-flowered and grey-leaved plants. Daisy blossom *Anthemis cupaniana* and the starry *Iberis sempervirens* gather around the bench. There are flanking groups of lily of the valley, silver-leafed curry plant, *Helichrysum italicum serotinum* (syn. *H. angustifolium)*, and *Lamium maculata* 'White Nancy' beneath 'White Triumphator' tulips. A 'Weeping Silver Pear' is a focal point behind the bench, and a vast bush of white-flowered *Rosa* 'Nevada' and two standard white-flowered wisteria are beginning to open their blooms. At the end of the borders, opposite the white wisteria standards, are a pair of larger, purple-flowered wisteria grown as standards.

The other part of the garden devoted to white is filling with white scilla, *Campanula alba, Geranium renardii, Potentilla alba,* and a ground covering of white-flowered violas, and the feathered silvery mops of *Tanacetum densum amanum.*

The Red Border for which Hidcote is perhaps best known (after its tapestry hedges) relies on the bedding-out of many tender perennials such as dahlias, pelargoniums, and canna lilies. However, in May these have not been put in place, and it is possible to study the permanent planting that provides much of the darker, muted shades of red and violet that give substance to the more vivid shades later in the season.

Acer platanoides 'Crimson King', *Prunus cerasifera* 'Atropurpurea' and Nigra, *Corylus maxima* 'Purpurea', and purple-leaved sage are just a few of the most obvious trees and shrubs. Even the coppery red tips of the *Pinus mugo* branches make their contribution, as does the architectural foliage plant *Rheum palmatum* 'Atrosanguineum'. Pink-flowered symphytum, *Ajuga repens* 'Atropurpurea', and *Heuchera sanguinea* 'Palace Purple' make ground-covering clumps between red and purple tulips and fiery double poppies 'Beauty of Livermere'.

The ranks of the blues and yellows of Mrs. Winthrop's Garden are reinforced with curling tendrils of golden hops winding through tripods set in the corners before the copper beech hedges screening the southern edge of this enclosure. *Lonicera nitida* 'Baggesen's Gold' adds its bright foliage to contrast the azure blue tussocks of viola 'Ullswater' and early sprays of delphiniums and bluebells.

From Mrs. Winthrop's, framed by the copper beech hedges, the view of Westonbirt beckons beyond the Stream Garden. Fuchsia-pink Asiatic primulas and the excellent young foliage of hostas, glaucous blue and variegated creamy white, cut across the middle ground, pulling the eye into the woodland. *Acer pseudoplatanus* 'Brilliantissimum', *A. palmatum*, and flowering Oshima cherry are the early show in Westonbirt.

Hidcote has many fine specimens of magnolia, including *M. thompsoniana*, *M. soulangiana* 'Rustica Rubra', *M. denudata*, and several *M. campbellii mollicomata*, all to be enjoyed throughout the early spring. But in June, the exquisite *Magnolia sinensis* is flowering in the south border of the Old Garden. This is from Szechuan province and has the most glorious pendant flowers with a wonderful lily-of-the-valley perfume. A self-sown seedling of this tree has been lifted and moved to the Lower Stream Garden to grow along a path. Such a plant must be placed where its fragrance can be enjoyed and its pendant flowers seen to their best advantage.

The remaining beds of the Old Garden seem to be given over to mauve and yellow: centaurea, thalictrum, phlomis, potentilla, *Rosa rubrifolia*, rose 'Lavender Pinocchio'—the flowers of which are a curious tea-stained lavender color—astrantia, hesperis, and *Deutzia × elegantissima*, which has mahogany-brown stems carrying fragrant shell-pink flowers.

The Bathing Pool in June is ringed with the blue-flowered poppy *Meconopsis × sheldonii* 'Branklyn', the finest of the hybrids of *M. betonicifolia* and *M. grandis*.

These bold broad flowers are perfectly complemented by the tiny blue dots of *Brunnera macrophylla*.

Peonies, Hidcote's other specialty, can be seen in wide variety in the Pillar Garden and in the border between the Rose Walk and the Old Orchard. Most impressive is the tree peony 'Souvenir de Maxime Cornu', with vast yellow flowers edged with carmine and heavily fragrant. *Azalea pontica* and philadelphus are flowering and perfuming the air, and the early specie roses begin to herald the imminent show of old shrub roses. Under the fading lilac blossoms, the drumstick stalks of *Allium aflatunense* carry mauve flower umbels that contrast with the peachy pink tones of lupin spikes and the blossoms of the pale damask rose 'Mme. Plantier' and centifolia roses in variety.

In the Garden Yard, the old farm buildings that now serve as garden stores are smothered in the honey-spice-scented racemes of *Wisteria floribunda* 'Microbotrys'.

July is the season for perfume at Hidcote, and the hedge-walled rooms hold the scent of sweetbriar foliage, mock orange, curry plant, and regal lily.

Wistaria floribunda 'Macrobotrys' cascades across the front of one of the old farm sheds in the Garden Yard behind the manor house, 2008. Ethne Clarke

The hedge of 'Rosa Mundi' around the kitchen garden is covered in flowers, and the new growth of the yew hedges shines bright green between the twinning strands of *Tropaeolum speciosum* that carry its flowers like tongues of flame into the dark yew.

The individuality of the color areas can be seen most clearly on a warm July day. The Rose Walk is softly tinted with shades of lavender-blue hebe, nepeta, and penstemon, dusty-pink roses, dianthus, and phlox with random highlights of white and pale yellow daisies. The somber color of the path is intended to serve as an undistracting foil for the subtle flower colors, and the present material replaces the original ash path that was even darker in color.

All garden studies must include a survey of the plantings that characterize the garden. In the case of Hidcote, one could concentrate on the enormous variety of choice specimen plants, or on the individual collections of plants that Major Johnston assembled. But Hidcote is a garden where the importance of the design is paramount, and the plants are used chiefly to support the layout, so we must look at associations, and the form, texture, and color of Hidcote's undeniably seductive planting schemes. Profusion and mass are key words to describe Johnston's approach to planting.

The little box-edged beds in the Maple Garden have been planted with heliotrope. Its fragrant deep purple flowers contrast their color and mingle their scent with that of the silver filigree leaf of *Artemisia* 'Powys Castle'. Cerise-pink pelargoniums, diascia, and Bordeaux-red knautia color the outer borders beneath the coppery foliage of *Acer palmatum*. *Magnolia stellata*, daphne, and choisya also grow here and in July contribute only background foliage, but indicate that in the earliest months of spring this small room near the house contains much flower and fragrance.

The Stream Garden is a virtual jungle, as all the ground-cover plants are at their fullest and the flowers of astilbe, astrantia, hosta, and *Lilium pardalinum* compete for attention with the elephant-eared foliage of *Gunnera manicata*, *Peltiphyllum peltatum*, and broad leathery strops of *Lysichitum americanum*.

Late Summer and Autumn

The glory of late summer at Hidcote is undoubtedly the Scarlet or Red Border. *Hemerocallis* 'Kwanso Flore Pleno', one of the first day lilies imported from Japan in 1864, is repeated in bold clumps along the front of each border. Its orange tint is picked up by *Lilium pardalinum*. Other repeat plantings are of *Cordyline australis*, *Phormium tenax* 'Atropur-pureum Nanum', and *Rheum palmatum*; these unify the borders and give structure to annual and perennial plantings, which can be divided into shades of red: *dahlias* 'Bloodstone' and 'Bishop of Llandaff'; *Canna indica* 'Le Roi Humbert'; *Lobelia cardinalis* 'Queen Victoria', 'Cherry Ripe', and 'Bees' Flame;' *Potentilla* 'Gibson's Scarlet'; *Verbena* 'Lawrence Johnston' and 'Huntsman'; *Geum* 'Mrs. Bradshaw'; *Heuchera americana*; annual lobelia; *Polygonium amplexicaule*; roses 'Frensham' and 'Super Star': and into shades of blue and purple: *Aconitum* 'Spark's Variety'; *Clematis viticella* 'Rubra'; deep purple sweet peas, buddleia 'Black Knight', and the foliage of trees and shrubs mentioned earlier.

In the Stream Garden, all is lush and green. Especially eye-catching

The Red Border in midsummer, 2008: a mix of shrubs, perennials, grasses, and bulbs selected for their red tints. Graham Stuart Thomas was instrumental in enhancing planting schemes at Hidcote to extend their season of interest and to make them more eye-catching. Andrea Jones

are *Dryopteris filixmas* and *Matteuccia struthiopteris*. These are excellent ferns, the former for anywhere shady except boggy ground and the latter for moist shade. Their fine foliage mixes well with the flowers of *Primula* 'Sutton's Blue' and 'Rowallane Rose', *P. pulverulenta* and *Astilbe* 'King Albert'.

As you pass into the Pillar Garden, the fragrance of lavender takes over. This whole end of the garden—the Stilt Garden (where *Salvia turkestanica* holds up its curiously scented steel-grey bracts above *Anchusa azurea* 'Loddon Royalist'), Terrace Garden, Cistus Bank, and Pillar Garden—is purely Mediterranean in feel. In the Pillar Garden, the peonies have been replaced by a sequence of sweetbriar roses with apple-scented foliage, and now *Romneya coulteri*, with many branched grey

The Red Border, c. 1988. Seymour Preston

stems and finely cut foliage, is rich with sweetly scented papery white flowers, as is the bold *Yucca flaccida*. At the foot of the Pillar Garden, the coloring moves from shades of mauve and silver into purples and rosy pinks with phlox and *Lavatera olbia* 'Rosea'.

Hidcote has an extensive array of hydrangea species and hybrids that are seen at their best in late summer, particularly in the areas around the Stream Garden and into Westonbirt. These include *Hydrangea aspera* 'Macrophylla', *H. serrata*, *H. sargentiana*, *H. paniculata* 'Grandiflora', and the loveliest, *H. villosa*. Walking along the paths to Westonbirt, plantings of hydrangeas and polygonatums have reached shoulder height and crown the way with felted foliage and mottled pink and white flowers.

In Westonbirt, as summer moves toward autumn, the berries and barks of the many specimen trees become most evident. Waxy red holly berries and the pinky pearls of *Sorbus vilmoranii* and *S. cuspidata* dangle above the orange-berried cotoneaster and berberis and scarlet and chocolate-brown rosehips on *Rosa pimpinellifolia* and *R. rugosa* 'Belle Poitevine' and 'Fru Dagmar Hastrup'. The peeling bark of *Betula ermanii*, *Acer griseum* underplanted with silver variegated *Lamium galeobdolon* 'Variegatum', and the striped green bark of *A. grosseri hersii* are especially noteworthy.

In the Stream Garden, the show is finally drawing to a close as the bold foliage plants begin to wither. Around the Bathing Pool, the racemes of *Cimicifuga racemosa* scent the air with a fragrance reminiscent of grape-flavored wine gums. *Gentiana asclepiadea*, the Willow Gentian, waves its royal-blue flowers at ankle height, and the white rose 'Iceberg' shines against the yews.

The beds of fuchsias are in full flower outside the Bathing Pool Garden, and in the White Garden, white-flowered nicotiana, *Potentilla alba*, *Anaphalis triplinervis*, and other common white flowers fill in between bushes of 'Gruss an Aachen' roses. At either side of the step up to the Cedar Lawn, *Cyclamen neopolitanum* are naturalizing to make carpets of rich pink over marbled green leaves.

In the borders of the Rose Walk, blue *Caryopteris clandonensis*, white Michaelmas daisies, and pink *Anemone japonica* have replaced the peach-

The pastoral scene outside Hidcote Manor Garden's sheltering walls, 2008. Andrea Jones

pink tones of rose and lupins. But the overall effect is still muted and contrasts with the ripening rosehips, the inky black berries on the *Viburnum rhytidophyllum* bushes on either side at the head of the walk, and the apples dropping in the orchard.

Throughout the year, species of geraniums, many types of symphytum and astrantia, ivies and hosta cover the ground in a weed-smothering blanket of foliage and flower. These and the constant strong shape of the many hedges give cohesion to the garden and its changing rhythms.

As a plantsman, Lawrence Johnston held his own with the best, and Hidcote was the source of many of our finest garden plants; these are just a few:

Campanula latiloba 'Hidcote Amethyst': A sport of 'Highcliffe', this is evergreen and bears delicate lilac-pink blooms; good for any soil in sun or shade.

Dianthus 'Hidcote': a clove-scented pink with dusty-rose flowers that makes clumps of typical grey-leaved foliage; needs well-drained soil in sun.

Hebe 'Hidcote': A pink-flowered hybrid of *H. speciosa*.

Hypericum 'Hidcote': A semi-evergreen, medium-sized shrub of compact habit. Its many golden saucer-shaped flowers appear from July to October. Will do well in all soils that have adequate drainage.

Jasminum polyanthum: An evergreen, it bears many pink-tinged waxy white flowers that are heavily scented and abound all summer. Johnston discovered this in China, and in 1941 it received an Award of Merit from the Royal Horticultural Society, followed in 1949 by a First-Class Certificate. It requires shelter and good soil.

Lavandula angustifolia 'Hidcote', 'Hidcote Giant', 'Hidcote Pink': All forms of the familiar lavender, perhaps collected by the Major when plant-hunting in the south of France.

Mahonia lomariifolia: Another of Johnston's introductions from China. Obviously, an evergreen with long leaves in pairs down stiff stems. It has an erect habit and the long flower racemes are held erect and covered in small bell-shaped flowers. Does best in semishade in a sheltered spot.

Penstemon 'Hidcote Pink': A really first-class salmon pink with strong flower spikes that carry on all summer. The plant needs full sun in well-drained soil. It is not reliably hardy but propagates easily from soft cuttings in early autumn.

Rosa 'Hidcote Gold': Described by Nancy Lindsay as a sport of *R. omietisis*, "brought from Yunnan by Major Lawrence Johnston in the 1930s, a gigantic briar with awesome ruddy-thorned canes and feathery fern-leaves of parrot-green; in blossom a corruscating cataract of sequins of candid gilt, in autumn a twinkle with a myriad coral-scarlet beads."

Rosa 'Lawrence Johnston': A plant Lindsay describes as "a graceful climber of shining april-green with clusters of shell-petalled chalices of glistening honey-yellow."

Symphytum 'Hidcote Pink' and 'Hidcote Blue': Self-explanatory varieties of excellent ground cover that today seem to have virtually taken over the garden of their origin.

Verbena 'Lawrence Johnston': A scarlet-flowered version of this tender plant, it has a prominent place at the front of the famous Hidcote borders.

BIBLIOGRAPHY

Blomfield, Sir Reginald, *The Formal Garden in England,* 1st edition. London: Macmillan, 1901; Waterstone, 1985.

Cameron, Roderick. *The Golden Riviera.* London: Weidenfeld & Nicolson, 1975; Editions, Limited, 1984.

Carruthers, Annette, *Ernest Gimson and the Cotswold Group of Craftsmen.* Leicestershire: Leicestershire Museums, Art Galleries, and Records Service, 1978.

Crowe, Dame Sylvia, *Garden Design.* Chichester: Packard Publishing, 1981; Garden Art Press, 1994.

de Navarro, Mary. *A Few More Memories.* London: Hutchinson & Co, 1936.

Girouard, Mark. *Sweetness and Light.* Oxford: Oxford University Press, 1977; Yale University Press, 1984.

Goode, Patrick, with Geoffrey Jellicoe, Susan Jellicoe, and Michael Lancaster. *The Oxford Companion to Gardens.* Oxford: Oxford University Press, 1986.

Gradidge, Roderick. *Dream Houses, the Edwardian Ideal.* London: Constable, 1980.

Hadfield, Miles, *A History of British Gardening,* London: J. Murray, 1979; Penguin, 1985.

———. *British Gardeners: A Biographical Dictionary.* London: Zwemmer Books, 1986; Zwemmer Books, 1986.

Hayward, Allyson, *Norah Lindsay: The Life and Art of a Garden Designer,* London: Frances Lincoln Ltd, 2007.

Jekyll, Gertrude, ed. *The Garden,* vol. 58, 1900.

Jekyll, Gertrude, ed. with Lawrence Weaver. *Gardens for Small Country Houses.* London: Country Life, 1911; Adamant Media Corporation, 2002.

Kemp, Edward. *How to Lay Out a Garden*. London: John Wiley & Son, 1901.

Lambert, Angela, *Unquiet Souls: The Indian Summer of the British Aristocracy, 1880–1918*. London: Macmillan, 1984.

Lees-Milne, James. *Ancestral Voices*. London: Chatto & Windus, 1975; Faber and Faber, 1984.

———. *Caves of Ice (Diaries, 1946 and 1947)*. London: Chatto & Windus, 1983; Faber and Faber, 1984.

Martineau, Mrs. Philip, *Gardening in Sunny Lands: the Riviera, California, Australia*. New York: D. Appleton & Company, 1924.

Masson, Georgina. *Italian Gardens*. London: Thames & Hudson, 1961; Antique Collectors' Club, 1987,

Mawson, Thomas, *The Art and Craft of Garden Making*. London: B. T. Batsford, 1901; Charles Scribner's Sons, 1926.

Muthesius, Hermann, with Dennis Sharp. *The English House*. New York: Rizzoli, 1979; Frances Lincoln Limited, 2007.

Newton, Ernest. *A Book of Country Houses*. London: B. T. Batsford, 1901.

Ottewill, David. *The Edwardian Garden*, New Haven: Yale University Press, 1989.

Pearson, Graham S. *Hidcote: The Garden and Lawrence Johnston*. London: Anova Books, 2007

Pereire, Anita. *Private Gardens of France*. London: Weidenfeld & Nicolson, 1983.

Racine, Michel, ed. *The Gardens of Provence and the French Riviera*. Boston: MIT Press, 1987.

Robinson, William, ed. *Flora and Sylva: A Monthly Review for Lovers of Garden, Woodland, Tree Or Flower; New and Rare Plants, Trees, Shrubs, and Fruits; the Garden Beautiful, Home Woods, and Home Landscape*. 3 volumes published 1903–5.

———. *Garden Design and Architects' Gardens*. London: John Murray, 1892.

Rockley, Alicia. *Historic Gardens of England*. London: Country Life, 1938.

Sales, John. *West Country Gardens: The Gardens of Gloustershire, Avon, Somerset, and Wiltshire*. Gloucester: A. Sutton, 1981; A. Sutton, 1981.

Scott, Geoffrey. *The Architecture of Humanism: A Study in the History of Taste*. London: Constable, 1914; W. W. Norton, 1999.

Sedding, J. D., with E.F. Russell. *Garden-craft Old and New*. London: Paul, Trench, Trübner & Company Ltd, 1891; Read Books, 2007.

Thomas, Graham Stuart. *The Art of Planting, Or, The Planter's Handbook*. Boston: David R. Godine, 1984.

———. *Cuttings from My Garden Notebooks*. New York: Sagapress, 1997.

———. *Gardens of the National Trust*. London: Weidenfeld & Nicolson, 1979.

Whalley, Robin. *The Great Edwardian Gardens of Harold Peto: from the archives of Country Life*. Aurum Press Ltd, London, 2007.

Wharton, Edith. *A Backward Glance* (reprint). London: Century Hutchinson, 1987; Read Books, 2007.

———. *Italian Villas and Their Gardens* (reprint). New York: Da Capo, 1976.

———. *Letters edited by R.W.B. Lewis & Nancy Lewis*. New York: Charles Scribner's Sons, 1988; also in the collection of the Beinecke Library, Harvard University.

Articles on individual gardens appear in back issues of *Country Life, The Garden* and other gardening periodicals. Listings for these can be found in Ray Desmond's *The Bibliography of British Gardens*, St Paul's Bibliographies, London, 1984.

INDEX